Flirting
FOR
DUMMIES®

by Elizabeth Clark

John Wiley & Sons, Ltd

Flirting For Dummies®

Published by
John Wiley & Sons, Ltd
The Atrium
Southern Gate
Chichester
West Sussex
PO19 8SQ
England

E-mail (for orders and customer service enquires): cs-books@wiley.co.uk

Visit our Home Page on www.wiley.com

For general information on our other products and services, please contact our Customer Care Department within the U.S. at 877-762-2974, outside the U.S. at 317-572-3993, or fax 317-572-4002.

For technical support, please visit www.wiley.com/techsupport.

Wiley also publishes its books in a variety of electronic formats. Some content that appears in print may not be available in electronic books.

British Library Cataloguing in Publication Data: A catalogue record for this book is available from the British Library

ISBN: 978-0-470-74259-4

Printed and bound in Great Britain by TJ International, Padstow, Cornwall

10 9 8 7 6 5 4 3

WILEY

About the Author

Elizabeth Clark, a.k.a 'the Flirt Guru', is an international speaker, broadcaster, author, and trainer. She is the UK's leading expert on flirting and charisma in business and the author of both *Flirt Guru* and *Single to Settled*.

Elizabeth is a member of the Professional Speakers Association, holds MCIPD and BPS qualifications, and possesses over 10 years of human resources management experience with FTSE-listed companies. Whilst there are no formal qualifications required to be a 'flirting expert', Elizabeth professes to have a lifetime of practical application behind her!

As the founder of Rapport Unlimited and www.flirtguru.com (in 2002), Elizabeth has engaged with tens of thousands of people around the globe from FTSE-listed clients. She provides corporate training and carries out speaking work, teaching flirting skills from persuasive presentation to charismatic networking. In doing so, Elizabeth has proved that skills used in flirting, for business or pleasure, are inextricably linked, and that flirting isn't just for dummies!

Elizabeth's cross-demographic appeal sees her feature in everything from *The Times* to *Grazia*. She appears regularly on radio and TV, from BBC1 to Living.

For more information on Elizabeth's work and for more flirting tips, visit her websites at www.rapportunlimited.co.uk and www.flirtguru.com, or contact her directly at info@rapport unlimited.co.uk.

Dedication

To Calum, Lucy, and Glyn – my superstars.

Author's Acknowledgements

The *For Dummies* series isn't a global phenomenon by accident, and I'd like to thank the raft of *For Dummies* editors who made this book possible.

What makes this book extra-special is the contribution of the models. Not only do they provide invaluable demonstrations, but they also add a touch of glamour to the book. I'd like to say a huge thanks to my best friend Patri Pennarocha and my gorgeous partner Glyn Powditch for their excellent modeling services, and to Bill Houston – our very patient, but brilliant photographer.

Thanks to my sister, Jo, for providing telephone stress relief, to all my clients for their support and encouragement whilst writing this book, and to my wonderful children, Calum and Lucy, who agreed to me writing another book, after I swore I wouldn't do another.

Publisher's Acknowledgements

We're proud of this book; please send us your comments through our Dummies online registration form located at www.dummies.com/register/.

Some of the people who helped bring this book to market include the following:

Acquisitions, Editorial,
and Media Development

Project Editor: Steve Edwards

Development Editor: Tracy Barr

Content Editor: Jo Theedom

Commissioning Editor: Nicole Hermitage

Publishing Assistant: Jennifer Prytherch

Copy Editor: Kate O'Leary

Proofreader: Helen Heyes

Technical Editor: Elizabeth Kuhnke

Executive Editor: Samantha Spickernell

Executive Project Editor: Daniel Mersey

Cover Photos: © Tetra Images/Getty Images

Cartoons: Rich Tennant
   (www.the5thwave.com)

Composition Services

Project Coordinator: Lynsey Stanford

Layout and Graphics: Reuben W. Davis

Proofreaders: Caitie Copple, David Faust

Indexer: Ty Koontz

Special Help

Brand Reviewer: Jennifer Bingham

Publishing and Editorial for Consumer Dummies

    Diane Graves Steele, Vice President and Publisher, Consumer Dummies

    Joyce Pepple, Acquisitions Director, Consumer Dummies

    Kristin A. Cocks, Product Development Director, Consumer Dummies

    Michael Spring, Vice President and Publisher, Travel

    Kelly Regan, Editorial Director, Travel

Publishing for Technology Dummies

    Andy Cummings, Vice President and Publisher, Dummies Technology/
    General User

Composition Services

    Gerry Fahey, Vice President of Production Services

    Debbie Stailey, Director of Composition Services

Contents at a Glance

Table of Contents

Introduction

*I*f you could learn one skill to improve your self-confidence and your listening skills, help you meet more people and project the right impression, and show you how to read and react to body language, not only would you want to learn it, you'd probably expect it to be on the curriculum in every school. Unfortunately, it isn't because this particular skill is flirting, and it has a bad press. Rather than being viewed as an essential social skill, flirting is viewed as something a bit grubby, sleazy, or for airheads simply because, in addition to making you friends and improving your relationships, it also gets you dates.

Without flirting, though, life would be duller, lonelier, and a lot less fun. Flirting's a great life skill that you can break down into logical elements, learn, and apply in all sorts of contexts from work to play.

Flirting is important for other reasons, too. A recent study showed that modern living places less value on community and the family unit than in previous generations. With a workforce shortage, everyone is encouraged to work, both young and old. People relocate more readily and commute farther to work than ever before, leaving less time and energy to spend on our families and friends. Children are being brought up by nurseries, instead of learning their communication skills at home around the dinner table with mum and dad.

A culture of alcohol sees teenagers relying on booze for their Dutch courage with the opposite sex rather than their communication skills. University, previously the place for a young person to hone their communication skills, as well as get lashed up at the expense of the taxpayer, is now a vehicle for accumulating debt. Nights on the town are replaced by nights working part time to make ends meet. All the key places and opportunities where you can learn to hone communication skills are changing, not necessarily for the better. Never mind the energy crisis, we're facing a communication skills meltdown and it's everyone's responsibility to do their bit. Honing your flirting skills is a way to reconnect lines of communication and engage with other people, despite all the social and economic forces pulling us apart. That's where this book comes in.

Each time you dip in and out of this book, something new and useful will stand out in your mind for your next flirting exploit. You'll become more likeable and attractive to others, learn how to spot the key signals, and act on them without the fear of rejection. You can teach an old dog new tricks – so get ready to put some work in and become a fabulous flirt.

About This Book

Flirting and courting are constantly practised in the animal kingdom. Surprisingly, we humans behave in much the same way. This book covers lots of information on how we behave, and why, in a simple, logical format that anyone can follow.

I elaborate on some of the more complex points using photographs. Illustrations are also provided to help you visualise and retain useful facts and information.

All the information is easy to access. You don't have to read the whole book to find solutions to your particular flirting difficulties. You can tailor make your own learning journey with the help of the index and the table of contents.

Conventions Used in This Book

This book is stereotype and jargon free. All the terms used here can be found in similar texts and contexts.

When this book was printed, some Web addresses may have needed to break across two lines of text. Where that happens, rest assured that I haven't put in any extra characters (such as hyphens) to indicate the break. So, when using one of these Web addresses, just type in exactly what you see in this book, as though the line break doesn't exist.

What You're Not to Read

You don't have to read any of the stories in the sidebars to understand the points made in the nearby sections. These sidebars are useful, though, to demonstrate a point and to reassure you that you're not the only person to experience flirting embarrassments or problems. Most of the stories have happy endings and so offer a bit of inspiration in your flirting development.

Nor do you have to follow the Try This icons, but you'll find your comfort zones will stretch more quickly and you'll get to your end goal faster if you do.

Foolish Assumptions

In writing this book, I've made some assumptions about you:

- ✔ You want to meet more people, improve your flirting skills, and have more confidence.

- ✔ You're willing to accept feedback and make changes.

- ✔ You're prepared to put in the work to develop your new skills.

One final word about assumptions: I tried not to make stereotypical assumptions in this book but I do think that men and women sometimes see things or do things differently – particularly when it relates to flirting! Research supports this rather commonsense view.

How This Book Is Organised

The great thing about the *For Dummies* books is that they're designed so you can dip in and out where you please at the parts you feel are most relevant or important for you, and this book is no exception.

Part I: Getting to Grips with Flirting Basics

Whether you're new to flirting or could do with a refresher, this part describes the origins of flirting and why it's all down to Mother Nature (and not some numbers game with a nasty script concocted by some cheesy chat-up merchant). This part reviews your current flirting approach and gets you in the right mindset to become a people magnet. I cover gender differences you need to be aware of and how to get things started with everyone from friends to colleagues to potential dates.

Part II: Getting Noticed! Making Contact

Getting noticed for all the right reasons is the first big step in the flirting process. In this part you find out how to look, sound, and smell fantastic and to make a head-turning entrance. Spotting who's up for a flirtation and who isn't is the second flirting step. I offer tips on making conversation effortlessly with anyone, anywhere. Being interesting to other people is the third step, which is actually far easier than it sounds.

Part III: Developing Killer Rapport with Body Language

You're moving into the non-verbal territory in this part. Contrary to popular belief, what you say isn't as important as how you say it. The chapters in this part cover how to project all the right signals to let people know how interested you are, make all the right noises without saying a word, spot the secret flirting clues that are specific to men and women, and learn how to spot a liar. Enjoy practising, offering, and interpreting the body language clues you need for successful flirting.

Part IV: Taking the Next Step

Things hot up in this part. Actions speak louder than words – so exit your comfort zone and just do it. Discover how to recognise the right time for making the next move, and how to take things further. The chapters in this part also cover rejection: how to let someone down gently and how to cope if someone makes it plain they don't fancy you.

Part V: The Part of Tens

The chapters in this part take a light-hearted look at opening conversational lines for every situation, flirting gaffes that can make or break a date, dealing with unwanted attention without causing a scene, and having fun and flirting safely.

Icons Used in This Book

To help you navigate your way through this book, I use a number of different icons:

Tips are practical pieces of advice for developing and honing your flirting skills in a particular area and actions you should take to help you achieve a certain level of flirting ability.

Beware of these points; they can make or break a flirting situation.

Commit these points to your memory for later use.

Fact icons highlight information relating to flirting, people, and behaviour.

Where to Go From Here

If you feel you already know the information in a certain section, skip to other sections that are more useful to you. You don't need to read this book from cover to cover, although getting the whole flirting picture and covering all your bases won't hurt.

I provide useful chapter and section cross-references throughout the book; so don't worry about missing vital information by not reading it systematically. Use the table of contents and the index to pinpoint what you're looking for; they also show you where else in the book you can find extra snippets on any given subject.

Beyond this book, I suggest you head straight to the nearest public place and get started. There's no time like the present – if you can't get out of the house, get on the phone or the Internet. Someone's out there just waiting for someone like you to give them a little sign that you'd like to get to know them better. Flirt for more friends, more confidence, and more dates.

If this book awakens an interest in reading non-verbal cues for more general use, check out *Body Language For Dummies* by Elizabeth Kuhnke. If you find change very difficult or a negative outlook impossible to overcome, try *Cognitive Behavioural Therapy For Dummies* by Rob Willson and Rhena Branch. Changing your outlook enables you to get the most from this book.

Part I
Getting to Grips with Flirting

"I don't know about the perfume or the dress,
but the duck call is working wonders."

In this part . . .

*T*his part contains all the fundamentals of flirting you need, as well as info on how to fix your flirting approach. I aim to make you ready and motivated to get out there and start mixing it up with friends, colleagues, and potential dates.

Chapter 1

The Making of a Successful Flirt

In This Chapter

▶ Understanding the fundamentals of flirting

▶ Recognising and sending flirting signals

▶ Putting yourself in the flirting zone

Mother Nature has blessed you with all the skills you need to be a super flirt. Perhaps you've lost touch with these skills along the way or haven't used them enough to have full confidence in them, but believe me you do have the skills and you can improve them to whatever degree you desire.

Flirting is a subtle combination of body language, confidence, attitude, and appearance. You can employ these features of your character to flirt in different ways, from the innocent, non-sexual, mutual kind of flirting where you're not attracted to the other person to full-on flirting when you're madly attracted to someone. Flirting's not just about sex, although that is a very pleasant by-product when the feeling's mutual, but about making personal connections with people you find interesting and want to get to know.

When you flirt with someone they feel good about themselves, and in return you feel good too. Being flirted with is the ultimate confidence booster and it's free.

If you've ever felt that a chapter out of your flirting life felt more like 'How to lose friends and alienate people', then your flirting exploits are just about to make a huge paradigm shift.

Flirting Fundamentals

For most people, the big flirting concerns are:

✔ How do I get people to notice me?

✔ How can I tell if they fancy me?

✔ What am I going to say?

✔ How do I move things on from being just friends?

I cover all of these issues in this book. What you need to know now are some of the basic principles that apply to flirting, explained in the following sections.

Tuning animal instincts

Flirting in the human and animal worlds has been studied by everyone from anthropologists to psychologists and you can use their findings to your benefit.

In the animal kingdom, the males are adorned with ornate tail feathers, impressive manes, or striking markings to attract a female. In humans, however, the situation's reversed: with the exception of the sixteenth and seventeenth centuries when men sported massive wigs and flamboyant clothing, women have taken on the role of prettying themselves to attract a mate.

Studies show that women initiate flirting 90 per cent of the time. Although men appear to do most of the running, they actually do so because women have invited their advances with their flirting signals.

In addition, both humans and animals follow species-specific mating rituals and displays that the other members are familiar with. Human courtship follows a five-step pattern when you meet someone you're attracted to:

1. **You make eye contact.** A passing glance doesn't cut it; flirting requires a deliberate eye contact that's held long enough for the other person to definitely notice.

2. **You smile.** Smiling shows you have an interest and is a non-verbal way to invite someone's attention.

3. **You preen a bit.** Arranging your hair, smoothing your clothes, and positioning yourself on your best side catches the attention of interested parties.

4. **You build rapport.** Disclosing personal information about yourself and asking questions about the other person accelerates the attraction process.

Disco dummy

Jake went to his first ever school disco. He'd looked up some tips online and spoken to his big brother about meeting girls. He came back with his ego deflated. 'I flirted at loads of girls and none of them were interested,' he told his mother. 'What made you think they were interested in the first place?' she asked. 'Nothing, I just fancied them, so I flirted at them,' he replied. Jake was lucky enough to have a mum that could give him the lowdown on how girls think and his next disco was much more successful.

Jake made a schoolboy error that many men continue to make throughout their adult lives. First, you need to find someone who's available; then you flirt with them, not at them. To be a successful flirt, look for the signs and follow your instincts.

5. **You find reasons to touch both yourself and the other person.** Touching yourself in autoerotic gestures and touching them at moments of increased rapport lets them know you're interested.

Follow your animal instincts to attract more friends and lovers. If you want to attract the opposite sex, emphasise your sexual differences; to discourage an attraction, downplay your differences.

Flirting: A game of two halves

It takes two to flirt. You can't flirt *at* someone; to have any chance of success, you flirt *with* them. Flirting with someone is like dancing: the movements are co-ordinated, but different.

In general, your role in and success with a romantic flirtation is determined by your gender. Women's success with men is directly related to their ability to send out courtship signals and to interpret how they reciprocate. Men's success with women relies on their ability to read the signals being sent to them, as opposed to being able to initiate their own flirting rituals. Both women and men need to accurately interpret the signals they receive and respond accordingly.

Men's difficulties in finding mates result from their lack of perception in reading women's signals; women's lie in not being able to find men who match their ideals. Guys start paying more attention; girls, stop being so fussy!

Flirting to attract new friends can be daunting because of the tendency to wait for the other person to make the move to engage you. However, that other person could well be employing the same tactic. Taking the initiative yourself is therefore the best and most successful way to meet new people and make new friends.

Attracting more friends through flirting is almost risk free and has a high success rate. Naturally, people are going to be attracted to you if you demonstrate all the key flirting signals, but in friendly proportions.

Common flirting pitfalls

Flirting has four common pitfalls that most of us have fallen into at one time or another:

- ✔ **Picking the wrong person to flirt with.** The key to flirting success is flirting with someone who's available. Too many people make the mistake of flirting with someone without first looking for clues that they'll be receptive to the attention.

- ✔ **Not knowing how to make the approach.** Dithering and procrastination kick in because you're not sure how to make an approach or what to say. Always approaching from the front and learning to use general conversation cues are the simple fixes for this problem.

- ✔ **Worrying that something awful will happen.** Fearing rejection is quite natural, but you can learn to overcome this fear, which in turn eradicates irrational fears of something awful happening.

- ✔ **Not being able to accurately read the signals you receive.** How can you respond appropriately if you misinterpret the signals coming your way? Actually, you can't. Misreading signals is one of the main reasons flirtations go awry. You can solve this problem by learning how to read body language.

Men have between 10 and 20 times more testosterone than women and as a result tend to view things in terms of sex. Research shows that men find it difficult to interpret subtle signs and nuances and can often mistake friendliness for sexual availability.

Getting in Tune with Body Language

Body language is a fundamental part of flirting because it shows how available, attractive, enthusiastic, and sexy we are, or are not.

Some signals are unconscious, so you have no control over them and nothing to learn; others are deliberate, so you need to put your best effort into learning them.

Being able to interpret other people's body language and actions provides you with clues to their emotions. You can use this information to tell when someone fancies you and also to build relationships at work and socially.

Becoming a people watcher

Nothing's more fascinating than people. The more you watch people, the more you learn about their behaviour and can predict how they'll react in certain situations. For this reason, companies spend small fortunes on psychometric testing to see if they can predict how someone is likely to behave in an occupational setting before hiring or promoting them. The added value you have over any test is that you can actually observe people in their own environment. You can learn to anticipate or predict behaviour in family and friends, as well as potential dates.

Get to grips with the behaviour of others and then strangers won't seem frightening figures that can make you feel awkward in their presence.

Next time you think 'X makes me uncomfortable' or 'I really enjoy bumping into Y', analyse why that's so. Consider what it is about their behaviour that makes you so uncomfortable or brightens up your day.

People-watching opportunities exist all around you, so make the most of them.

Spotting key signals in other people

Being able to recognise the right signals gives you the confidence to step up to the flirting mark. You can tell whether someone's initiating a flirtation if they do the following: make eye contact, smile at you, fiddle with their clothing or hair, initiate a conversation or mirror your behaviour, or find reasons to touch you. These behaviours are the same five outlined in the human courtship pattern mentioned in the earlier section 'Tuning animal instincts'. If you see them, you're good to go. For the full rundown on flirting signals, see Chapters 10, 11, and 12.

Right clues, wrong order

Dave had researched flirting behaviour and had made a checklist of what to look for when he met a woman to see if she fancied him. The signs were:

1. Dilated pupils

2. Swollen lips

3. Batting eyelashes

4. Moist, dewy eyes

5. Hair flicking

Dave was most upset that none of the women he fancied showed any signs of fancying him; in fact, they couldn't get away fast enough.

Dave's checklist wasn't bad, however. His mistake was just marching up to women and checking if they were all in evidence. Dave returned to the drawing board and included all the initial signals which he'd thought were a bit boring and general, and before he knew it he'd bagged himself a dream date.

Flirting follows a process. Checking to see if you've made a good cake is useless if all the ingredients are just heaped into a tin and thrown in the oven. You start with the ingredients, mix them in the right order with the correct tools, pop the tin into a pre-heated oven – and bingo you get something hot and tasty.

Looking at revealing behaviour

Our gestures are created by our emotions. Being aware of the gestures we can control as well as those that are involuntary provides a good picture of what gives your hand away, as well as what holds you back.

Our emotions are most commonly revealed by the:

- ✔ **Face:** Even if you have great control over your face, minuscule movements still occur before you have time to compose yourself. The skilled eye can thus see your feelings 'written all over your face'. (See Chapter 10 on interpreting the facial language code.)

- ✔ **Hands:** Because the hands are in front of the body they're beautifully placed to be observed. Trying to hide your hands may make you appear deceptive. Wringing your hands shows anxiety and rubbing your palms slowly together makes you look as if you're up to something, but if they're relaxed and open they show that you're comfortable in a person's company. (See Chapter 11 on using your hands.)

Flirting monolith

You couldn't knock Jess back with an iron bar. She was undoubtedly the best flirt that any of her friends had ever come across. They were dissecting her 'secret' one night over a drink. Without being unkind, she wasn't the best-looking girl, was on the short side and rather plump. Short of hypnotising men, they struggled to understand Jess's phenomenal hit rate. What they were overlooking was that Jess:

✔ Smiled a lot

✔ Made good eye contact

✔ Was friendly with everyone

✔ Could read men like a book

✔ Was an expert in using all the female flirting signals

✔ Didn't let the odd knock-back upset her

Jess just didn't care what people thought of her. She presented the best impression she could and people loved her for it. From the paper shop to the pub, her energy and vitality won everyone over.

Being a successful flirt takes energy and resilience. Treat every encounter as a flirtation in the making. If it doesn't work out, get looking for the next opportunity, but never let the odd rejection stop you.

> ✔ **Feet:** As your feet are farthest away from your brain you have less control over them, making them very revealing. Your feet tend to point in the direction you want to be heading: point them towards someone and you want to be with them; point them away and chances are you'd rather be somewhere else.

Next time you're talking to someone and you'd rather not be, check in which direction your feet are pointing.

Face, hands, and feet provide a simple means of interpreting revealing behaviour. Complement this understanding with tips on rapport building in Chapter 8 to give yourself a great head start.

Getting Yourself in the Flirting Mindset

Question: What would you attempt if you thought you couldn't fail?

Answer: Anything.

The end is nigh

Jane would rather do nothing than do something because she was convinced that whatever she tried would go wrong. She always wore trousers when she went out, and when her friends tried to coax her into buying a dress, she refused point blank. 'My mum says I have horrible legs and I can't wear a dress as I'll make a show of myself,' was her twisted reasoning. It turned out that Jane's mother didn't have a positive word to say about anything or anybody. Jane had lived with her mother's negativity hanging over her, conditioned into thinking that she was useless and worthless. Jane's friends made a pact to stop her using negative phrases at the ends of sentences; they also said positive things to her about her appearance and her personality. Jane eventually felt positive enough to buy a dress and she looked great in it. Having the confidence to make a change also made her more confident in herself. Instead of viewing the men she met in bars with cynicism, she started to give them a bit of a chance. Before she knew it, Jane was accepting compliments from a stranger about her dress and she didn't attempt to deflect them or to put herself down. Jane managed to put a lifetime of negative conditioning behind her and is now in a stable relationship.

If someone like Jane can grasp the positivity initiative, anyone can. Just think of the rewards and stay focused on becoming the brilliant flirt you are.

To be a brilliant flirt you have to approach it as though you can't fail. Obviously not every flirtation is going to go exactly to plan, but learning from your errors is all part of the process. Remember: flirting's about having attitude; if you believe you can do it, you can. If your fears of rejection are getting in your way, overcome them with help from Chapter 15.

Practise flirting every day, with people of all ages and with both men and women. Mastering the innocent mutual kind of flirting first is an important step to take to enable you to successfully conquer the full-on variety.

Setting your thinking

You have the power to control your thoughts, although sometimes it can feel quite the opposite.

If you hear enough negative messages, you believe them. Telling yourself that you're useless or can't do something becomes a self-fulfilling prophecy. You need to change your thinking. Throughout the book you'll find tips for putting together mantras or positive *affirmations*. These are just simple little messages or phrases you keep repeating to yourself to align your subconscious with your positive way of thinking.

Make the choice to be a brilliant flirt and look forward to reaping the rewards with more friendships, better working relationships, and great dates.

Each night, just before you go to sleep, get rid of your automatic negative thoughts. Replace these thoughts with three things that you've done well that day. Focus on what you've achieved and stamp out the negatives. This process is even more effective if you take a few moments to write down your successes. The following morning, review your notes and congratulate yourself.

Banishing flirting baggage

Flirting baggage is all the bad experiences we carry with us that convert into negative feelings and effectively stop us from fulfilling our flirting potential. Banishing your flirting baggage is a must before you rebuild your lovely flirting skills. Two types of baggage exist:

- **The type that you tell people about.** Your mother told you not to air your dirty laundry in public for a reason. Not only are people uncomfortable hearing about it, this baggage reflects negatively on you, regardless of what the problem is or who was to blame.

  Never mention your ex-partners or hang-ups when you first meet someone; let them form their own opinion. Put all your energy into how you sound, not what you say. See Chapter 5 for tips on making yourself sound confident.

- **The type that you harbour inside you.** If your baggage has been going round in your mind for a while, you've probably blown it out of all proportion. This baggage isn't as bad as you think it is, and it certainly isn't important to the new flirtations in your life. They're flirting with you to get to know you better, not to get to know your life history of hang-ups. You're going to replace your baggage with new experiences with your new flirtations – time to move on.

Think about the last time you saw someone you fancied; did any nagging doubts about your flirting prowess or previous relationships prevent you from talking to them? Don't let your inhibitions or past experiences thwart your flirting ambitions. When you have told a new flirtation about your ex or previous failed relationships, have they looked delighted? Did they ask to see you again? If you answer 'No' to these questions, you need to get a grip on flirting conversation – Chapter 8 has lots of tips.

Second base, here we come

Seb had dated lots of women, but had never made it past first base. This would have been disappointing enough in itself, but he felt the need to explain his failure to every woman he dated, just to complete his humiliation and put her in the picture about his dating immaturity. Seb's mates set him up a blind date and gave him strict instructions not to give her the flirting death knell speech about his lack of conquests. They got on really well and went on to dates two, three, and four. Eventually, Seb confessed that he was very nervous about the whole sex thing. By now Anne was extremely fond of him and, although she laughed, she was very understanding. They're now married with two kids.

Let people get to know you for who you are and not in relation to your baggage to give your flirtations the best possible start.

Spotting daily opportunities

Feeling more positive about making more friends and getting more dates with your shiny new attitude? All you need now are opportunities to let yourself loose.

Practice makes perfect; use a range of flirtations regularly to become a flirting expert.

Think about your daily routine and the types of people you're likely to encounter through the course of a day. You're looking for lots of friendly flirting opportunities to cut your teeth on and boost your confidence and skills, as well as more adventurous romantic flirtations.

In an average day you can expect to interact with:

- People in queues, in shops, banks, cafes, and so on
- People on public transport
- Commuters in traffic jams and at traffic lights
- Colleagues at work
- People at the gym or involved in your chosen hobby/interest
- People via email
- People by text
- People on forums or in chatrooms

Ho, ho, ho

Barbara went to the local theatre to collect her daughter from her dance school's show. As she waited in the foyer for the performance to finish, Santa approached her. He showed her the split in the back of his trousers and asked if she thought the children would be able to notice it. Santa's young face was just as cute as his bum, and Barbara couldn't help but engage in a mild flirtation with him.

Santa was quite happy to reciprocate; he was terrified of facing 200 screaming kids and it was a pleasant distraction from his pre-stage nerves. In the space of a few minutes Barbara and Santa enjoyed a delicious – and innocent – flirtation. It left Barbara with a smile on her face and Santa with a spring in his step.

Never miss the opportunity to make someone else's day with a friendly flirtation, be they young, old, or the same sex as you.

✔ Parents at the school gates

✔ People dog walking

✔ People shopping

The list of opportunities is endless, so you've no excuse not to practise your flirting on a daily basis.

To find out more about exploiting your opportunities, see Chapter 4 on flirting with friends, dates, and colleagues, and Chapter 6 on spotting who's available.

Chapter 2

Identifying Your Flirting Style and Making It More Effective

• •

• •

*I*dentifying your flirting style is a great opportunity to reflect on the most successful parts of your flirting skills as well as identifying the aspects that perhaps aren't working as well as they could be or are even holding you back. Discovering which tricks make your flirting icons so successful with the opposite sex also helps you reinvent yourself as the kind of flirt you've always aspired to be!

Understanding Your Flirting Style

If you look hard enough when you're out and about, you can identify a whole host of different flirting styles. In this section, I look at four of the most common styles.

The minesweeper

A minesweeper trawls every room in a building for potential targets to flirt with, and is never happier than when laying on the charm. The problem for the minesweeper is being taken seriously by potential dates when wanting something more serious.

The life and soul of the party

The life and soul of the party is never short of company – a magnet for people – and is someone that everybody loves. Being able to draw people in this way means that the life and soul of a party tends not to have to search out people to flirt with. The only problem with this is that if someone doesn't have the confidence to approach the life and soul of a party, that person falls under the flirting radar.

The quietly confident person

A quietly confident person knows they've got 'it', but is selective about when to use it and doesn't feel the need to be the life and soul. However, when quietly confident people give off signals only around people they find attractive, they give off the wrong signals to people who find *them* attractive and miss out on flirtations they didn't know existed.

The wallflower

The wallflower likes to watch everything going on but doesn't give off any flirting signals and hasn't yet built up the confidence to go out there and get stuck into the flirting action. The wallflower has a lot to offer but needs to learn to build up confidence.

Novice or a Pro? Gauging Your Flirting Acumen

To determine how 'skilled' you are at flirting, you need to look at two things: how confidently you flirt in both the workplace and in social environments and your ability to adapt your flirting style appropriately for maximum effect.

Evaluating your confidence level

To gauge how confident you are as a flirt, ask yourself these questions:

In professional interactions: When first meeting someone in the office that you find attractive, do you:

1. Look them in the eye and greet them with a cheery smile and a hello?

2. Look their way, but wait for them to make the first move to say hello?

3. Wait for someone else to make the introductions?

In social settings: When first meeting somebody socially that you find attractive, do you:

1. Catch their eye, then approach them confidently?

2. Catch their eye, then wait until they make the move or until you're absolutely sure it's safe to approach them?

3. Stand rooted to the spot hoping they'll notice you, then kick yourself when they leave for missing the opportunity to speak to them?

Here's how to interpret your answers:

- ✔ **If you answered both questions with 1s:** You're a pro on the confidence front; you'll never miss an opportunity. If you're not getting as many opportunities as you'd like, get out more.

- ✔ **If you answered both questions with 2s:** You're pointing in the right direction but need a little more conviction to get your flirting muscles flexing.

- ✔ **If you answered both questions with 3s:** You have the most potential for growth. Just follow the tips in this book and everything will start falling into place.

- ✔ **If you've got a mixed result:** You're more confident in one setting than the other. When it comes to flirting you have to use it or lose it, so put more effort into the area with the higher score and watch all your relationships flourish.

To further understand your confidence level, ask yourself the same questions but for someone to whom you're *not* attracted. Getting a smaller score (2s instead of 3s or 1s instead of 2s, for example) indicates that you're more confident flirting with people you're not attracted to and therefore less confident when you fear rejection. Take heart, though: I've never met anyone that relishes rejection, but by using all the steps in the book you'll be able to spot the key signs, minimise your chances of rejection, and flirt with confidence.

Evaluating your adaptability

A good flirt uses their interpersonal talents appropriately, in both the workplace and socially. Whether you're improving your working relationships, making friends or winning dates, the same skills are at play to a greater or lesser degree. By learning to play with the 'volume' control on the elements of your flirting skills, you can adapt your flirting appropriately regardless of the setting. For example, you wouldn't want your boss feeling as if you were hitting on them, and by the same token you wouldn't want a date to feel as if they were nothing more than a polite acquaintance.

You can judge your adaptability as a flirt by flirting with a friend the way you would flirt with a date and then seeing how they react. Do they:

1. Not notice?

2. Start to behave differently towards you?

3. Ask you why you're acting differently with them?

If the answer is 1: Your adaptability is low, and your friend hasn't registered your approach. You need to be more aware of how you behave towards and around different types of flirting scenarios.

If the answer is 2: Friends naturally mirror each other's behaviour and reflect actions. You can see from the changes in your friend's behaviour that they are reflecting the change in yours. Develop this further in other scenarios to see how your flirting volume changes.

If the answer is 3: Your approach has lacked subtlety and has triggered a response that hasn't mirrored your own actions. You need to look at your basic flirting skills and work on amplifying or toning them down depending on the situation.

Finding and Fixing the Flaws in Your Approach

Learning everything there is to know on a subject won't make you accomplished, but learning what *you* could do differently or better takes your performance to the next level. Casting a critical eye over yourself is never easy, but it's a great habit to acquire if you want to continually evolve and improve your flirting skills.

Analysing what's holding you back

Finding that little something that's stopping you from taking the risks you need to have greater flirting prowess is simply a case of looking for your constraints.

You may face the following constraints:

- ✔ **Time:** You don't have the time available to meet people.

- ✔ **Previous relationships:** If a previous relationship failed, you're concerned another relationship may go the same way.

- ✔ **Friends and family:** They may prefer to have you at their beck and call and without the complication of a partner/date.

- ✔ **Money:** You can't afford a new wardrobe and all the spending money to go dating.

- ✔ **Confidence:** You don't feel able to flirt with new people.

- ✔ **Appearance:** You're not happy with your appearance; you want to lose some weight or buy some new clothes before you meet anyone.

 Write down a list of all your constraints. You'll be amazed by how many constraints you can come up with when you feel reluctant or wary. Identifying your constraints is the first step on the way to challenging and overcoming them.

Cutting the apron strings

Bob had a place on his own, having separated from his girlfriend. His mother took to visiting him on Saturday nights, because he hadn't yet found a social circle that didn't involve his ex. Bob's mum found his company far preferable to that of his father, who'd snore and grunt his way through the Saturday night entertainment on TV. She'd make life as comfortable as possible for Bob, making his favourite meals and bringing the latest films to watch together.

Eventually Bob decided it was time to get out before he turned into his father. By now his mother was well into her new weekend regime and resented the change. She went out of her way to keep him at home with her, even letting herself in ready to meet Bob and any new lady friend he happened to bring home for coffee.

It was tough, but Bob managed to cut the apron strings and motivate himself away from a life of Saturday night TV and a hearty meal with his mum, towards getting out and meeting some new faces. Still traumatised by the experience with his mother, Bob enjoys dating but won't be settling into anything serious for a while.

To get out and get flirting, you need to challenge your constraints and gather your motivation.

Looking at your motivation

Motivation is crucial for becoming more flirtatious. Motivation generally falls into two camps:

- ✔ **People who are motivated *towards* something:** These people take the risks because they want a relationship.

- ✔ **People who are motivated *away* from failure:** People in this camp won't approach anyone because they don't want to make a fool of themselves.

These types of motivation, either 'towards' or 'away', won't only be manifested in your flirting ability; they'll also be reflected in your attitudes towards money (you invest money because you want to make a return, or you save money because you don't want to risk losing it) and work (you aim for the job of your dreams or you stick with the job you've got and hope that a promotion eventually comes along).

To be able to flirt spontaneously, you need to work on changing your motivation. Every flirtation you have could lead 'towards' something great, from making a new friend to getting a date. On the 'away from' setting, it could be that every flirtation you have takes you one step further 'away from' loneliness.

Whichever way you look at it, motivation's necessary to get you flirting more.

Applying the 80:20 rule to improve your approach

A clever bloke called Pareto developed the 80:20 rule, which basically says that 80 per cent of problems can be solved by 20 per cent effort. This principle can be applied to many things. In a recent fight with my other half over time constraints, we agreed that many of them could actually be solved by hiring someone to do all the things we don't have time to – 80 per cent of the problems solved by one relatively easy action – much quicker than actually splitting all the chores and doing them ourselves, with the added bonus that we can be getting on with other things.

By applying the same approach to the constraints that inhibit your flirting, you can make great progress. Rather than tackle every little thing individually, which would essentially delay your chance to make the most of your flirting opportunities, you could fix one thing that would lead to the biggest gains for yourself. To do this, take your list of constraints and categorise them from the biggest flirting inhibitor to the smallest. Give each constraint a weighting of between 1 and 100, with the total value of all the constraints adding to 100. Pick the biggest value constraint and put your efforts into overcoming it.

Influencing your subconscious

Your subconscious is a funny thing; it listens to you all day then takes what you've said and repeats it back to you when you're asleep. The subconscious doesn't have a sense of humour and takes everything you say literally. Even if you joke with someone that your backside's big or that you're not handsome enough, when you're asleep at night it comes to life and is horrified that your bum's big or that you're not handsome. It tells you that you've a huge rump and an ugly face. After a while when you look in the mirror, you're mortified to see that you have an enormous backside and a face that only a mother could love.

Using your subconscious to your advantage is very simple: only tell it good things and it will gradually boost your confidence to giant proportions. Tell yourself that you're a fabulous catch and that any lucky person would be delighted to land you. Compliment yourself on all your best features and give yourself a pat on the back for everything you've done that day well before you go to bed.

Same figure, different perspectives

Patsy was a tall, attractive woman with no shortage of male admirers. However, she obsessed about her figure and managed to convince herself she was fat. Her friends continually assured her she had a great figure, but the self-doubt continued. One day in a gym class one of Patsy's friends looked in the mirror and noticed a tall, slim woman in the class. They were surprised to see that it was actually Patsy. Not only had she altered her own body image in her head, her negativity had also caused her friends to see her in the same way. After their shock at their altered image of Patsy, her friends insisted that no more negative talk be allowed and gradually even Patsy started to like what she saw in the mirror.

Be positive with yourself and the people around you to maintain your best possible self-image.

Changing Your Flirting Style

Resisting change is natural. Even if the change is welcome, you can still find it challenging. Maintaining changes you've made can be equally hard, but once you've established them as a way of life, they're just the way you do things.

If you're finding making changes difficult, write this mantra on a piece of paper and pin it to your bathroom mirror. Repeat it every time you see it and when you're finding changes difficult: 'If you always do what you've always done, you'll always have what you always had.'

Changing your flirting style and finding success happens much quicker if you actively do something to help. Reading this book is a start, but just like buying a lotion for curing baldness or cellulite, if it just sits in your bathroom cabinet you won't see any results.

Emulating someone you admire

Copying someone you admire – your flirting icon – is one of the simplest ways to improve your flirting style. Flirting icons aren't limited to the rich and famous; fabulous flirts are in action all around you. If you've worked with someone who always seems to effortlessly get their own way, or who's never short of company, or who relishes entertaining a crowd of people, then you've watched a supreme flirt in action. Mimicking their technique 100 per cent isn't always possible, but you can adapt their approach to suit your style.

Picking your flirting icon

When you pick your icon, do so with care. When I was tiny I loved watching Marilyn Monroe films. When I hit my teens, I borrowed my mother's lipstick and pouted through half-closed lids, huskily slurring my words. The effect wasn't quite what I'd hoped for – more punch drunk, pubescent teenager than sex idol. I quickly learned that when adapting a style, choosing someone more akin to your own personality and the times than a throw back from decades ago is best.

When choosing a flirting icon, you're not committing yourself to anything for life, only for as long as that icon is appropriate for you. Elvis may have been a great icon in his day, but you'd be getting attention for all the wrong reasons if you were trying to emulate him now. In our celebrity-obsessed culture, business professionals, entrepreneurs, film, music, and reality TV stars are all available icons. Just pick one you identify with.

Achieving the Joanna Lumley effect

Kate had always been confident in her flirting abilities and was able to get on with pretty much anybody. She was friendly, bubbly, and outgoing, and men loved her. However, she was constantly undermining her own confidence as a flirt because she perceived that she lacked sophistication.

She confided in a friend, whose opinion she valued, that if she could change anything, she'd like to be more sophisticated. Her friend asked her to explain exactly what she meant. 'I want to be like Joanna Lumley: calm, sophisticated, and lady-like,' Kate moaned. Her friend was shocked, and replied that she'd always considered Kate sophisticated because she carried herself so well and could flirt with anybody. Bolstered by her friend's revelation, Kate continued with her own brand of flirtatious sophistication and never let the thought undermine her again.

Before making any radical changes to your flirting style, seek the opinion of someone you trust.

Applying your icon's style

Having chosen your icon, determine what exactly it is about them you wish to emulate by deconstructing their style into the following areas:

- ✔ **Clothes:** What do you like about their attire? Is it the height of fashion (Posh and Becks), quirky (Russell Brand and Amy Winehouse), conservative (Tom Cruise and Katie Holmes), or casual (Brad Pitt and Angelina Jolie)?

- ✔ **Appearance:** Are they clean cut, grubby, immaculately groomed, or natural?

- ✔ **Body language:** Do they move in a confident, aggressive, flirtatious, gregarious, or considered way?

- ✔ **General demeanour:** Are they happy, aloof, well-grounded, formal, relaxed, friendly, or approachable? Does your icon, in an interview situation, smile and make good eye contact, remain composed but approachable, talk candidly on any subject, and so on?

By comparing your icon's style to your own, you can start to see areas that you need to modify. Chapter 5 gives you a great boost on working on your appearance, Chapter 7 helps you emulate their instant appeal, and Part III helps you replace your body language sins with star quality.

Making up for missed opportunities

Think back over the last month and count how many opportunities you missed to engage with someone (not just someone you fancy, but anyone of either gender); consider colleagues, friends, people in the street, or attractive strangers. Any one of those people would've felt better about themselves following a friendly exchange or flirtation, could've been the next link in the chain towards meeting your dream date, or could've actually been your dream date.

 If working out a month's worth of opportunities is a bit challenging for your memory, during your next 'typical' day, count the number of potential chances you have to make friendly contact – include anything from a smile, hello, or eyebrow flash (you can find out about eyebrow flashing and other ways to use your eyes to advantage in Chapter 7) – and multiply this number by 30 to get a good estimate.

Taking advantage of all those missed opportunities is the next step in ramping up your flirting abilities. Make a conscious decision to do something different.

This may sound counterintuitive, but if your total missed opportunities are zero or very few, then some lifestyle changes are needed. In other words, if you have few opportunities to capitalise on, you need to actually make some. You need to be around people to make yourself feel more human and involved (see Chapter 6 for ideas on where to find other singletons). Other ways to increase your flirting opportunities include taking a walk at lunchtime near a busy sandwich shop, joining a club (anything from badminton to energy conservation), or getting online and involved in a virtual community.

 Prioritise your opportunities into those you feel are the easiest to approach first. Eyebrow flashes (see Chapter 7 for more on these) are very easy on the comfort zone, as well as being non-sexual in intention, and are the most commonly reciprocated. Flash all your potential opportunities and you'll be surprised by the response rate.

 Try eyebrow flashing the big boss at work. They're the top dog because they're not only good at their job, they're also good with people (one would hope!). You'll start registering with them on a subconscious level and can build up your relationship with them as you work through the book.

Trapped

Julia was recently divorced, with a one-year-old child. She'd returned to work, for a sole trader, and her day involved dropping the baby with the childminder, going to her boss's office, beavering away on her own, with occasional appearances from her employer, collecting the baby on the way home, and being trapped in the house all evening with no babysitter and little company.

Undeterred, Julia bought herself a computer and got online. She met various people on everything from forums to dating sites. She loved being able to 'chat' with people who had the same interests as her without the awkward introductions; she could just slip into a group and be part of it. She met a couple of the men she'd been chatting to, but felt no spark, despite being attracted to their online personas. Eventually, she met a guy with whom she had mutual chemistry, and five years down the line she has lots of online friends and is getting married.

You can always meet new people and find your perfect partner; you just have to create opportunities where they don't already exist.

Taking more risks

Comfort zones are good – they're comfortable after all, but limiting. If you want to improve your skills you have to be prepared to go further and take risks. Clearly I'm not talking about putting yourself in danger here, simply testing your comfort zone and growing it as a result. The most common risk when trying to communicate with people is that they're going to reject or ignore your efforts. Ramping up your efforts in the right order not only builds your confidence, you suddenly find yourself surrounded by friendly opportunities. The risk scale in Figure 2-1 shows which ways of communicating have most and least risk.

Setting yourself flirting challenges

Getting results requires challenges. To get results in a diet, for example, you have to set targets; most diets initially aim for a 10 per cent loss in your body weight. Why not use that figure as a target to improve your flirting? For great flirting results, look to hit 10 per cent of your flirting opportunities with an eyebrow flash, smile, and greeting in your first few days. If you have ten opportunities a day, a 10 per cent improvement means you have to connect with just one person.

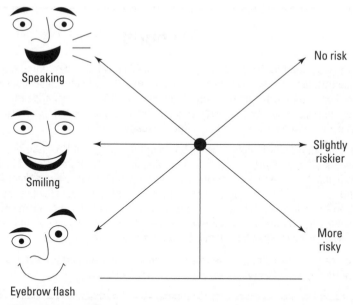

Speaking

Smiling

Eyebrow flash

No risk

Slightly
riskier

More
risky

Figure 2-1: Scale of risk.

Once you find flashing, smiling, and greeting comfortable, set your-self more advanced targets, such as:

✔ **Getting to know more about the person you're flirting with.** Head to Chapter 8 for details on making conversation with anybody.

✔ **Asking them out.** Chapter 13 tells you how.

Reading the flirting thermometer

A scale of flirting hotness exists. If you're playing it too cool, people won't be able to tell if you're flirting or not. If you go in too hot too quickly, you may come across as over-eager. Mastering the scale helps you recognise when someone is having a flirtation with you and also enables you to give them the right signs back to ensure your flirtation goes down smoothly. Figure 2-2 shows the hotness scale, along with references to chapters where you can find out more:

✔ **Icy:** Avoid this temperature at all costs if you're not to appear aloof or austere, like all the people you consider aloof, stuck up, or generally a bit miserable.

✔ **Cool:** This level can and should be applied to every person you meet, regardless of age or gender. Playing it cool means applying the basics to let someone know that you like them – smiling, eye contact, and the initial groundwork for a full-on flirt.

✔ **Getting warmer:** This level provides you with an idea of the sorts of things you need to be doing to let the other person know that you're ready for a good flirt.

✔ **Hot:** When you're 'hot' and the other person is showing all the same signs, you're good to go and have achieved the flirting holy grail!

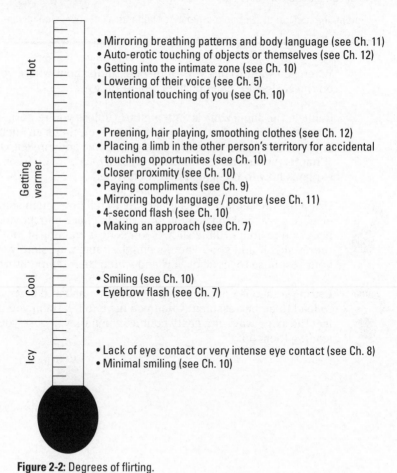

Hot
• Mirroring breathing patterns and body language (see Ch. 11)
• Auto-erotic touching of objects or themselves (see Ch. 12)
• Getting into the intimate zone (see Ch. 10)
• Lowering of their voice (see Ch. 5)
• Intentional touching of you (see Ch. 10)

Getting warmer
• Preening, hair playing, smoothing clothes (see Ch. 12)
• Placing a limb in the other person's territory for accidental touching opportunities (see Ch. 10)
• Closer proximity (see Ch. 10)
• Paying compliments (see Ch. 9)
• Mirroring body language / posture (see Ch. 11)
• 4-second flash (see Ch. 10)
• Making an approach (see Ch. 7)

Cool
• Smiling (see Ch. 10)
• Eyebrow flash (see Ch. 7)

Icy
• Lack of eye contact or very intense eye contact (see Ch. 8)
• Minimal smiling (see Ch. 10)

Figure 2-2: Degrees of flirting.

Desperate Dan

Dan was rather dishy, with no shortage of admirers. However, the women he dated never really made it into a proper relationship. They had one complaint in common: they couldn't tell what Dan thought of them and so dropped out rather than risk getting dumped.

Dan was at a loss as to how to proceed until he discovered the flirting thermometer. Using this guide, he increased his temperature for those women he really liked and looked for responsive changes in them. He also used it in his business relationships to ensure he projected the right signals to clients.

Getting the hang of the flirting thermometer benefits all of your relationships.

When you want to flirt with someone, think about where you fall on the scale and then consider where they are.

Being in the same zone is a great start (unless you're both icy). If the other person's hotter than you, however, that's an encouraging sign, but you need to increase your game and move up a gear. (Chapter 11 covers how to use body language and Chapter 12 explains how to recognise signs of flirting.)

 Using the thermometer is a great way to tell how much someone else likes you and to keep the situation in check and moving at a pace you're comfortable with. If someone is running at 'hot' on the thermometer and you're not feeling the same way, simply adjust your response to 'cool' or 'icy' and watch their temperature fall.

 Letting someone continue to flirt with you unabated is only going to lead to embarrassment when you have to tell them you don't feel the same way, or a nasty conflict when they accuse you of leading them on.

Chapter 3

Grasping the Gender Gap and Other Strategies for Flirting Success

In This Chapter

▶ Setting the girls apart from the boys

▶ Differing ends of the attractive spectrum

*T*o enjoy life as a successful flirt, you have to start treating the opposite sex as an opposite sex. While employers may like to pretend 'staff' means an androgynous mass of people, and reams of red tape enforce the concept, ultimately we're opposite sexes. From the office to the bedroom, different things make each gender tick and trying to pretend otherwise is flirting suicide. Embracing the differences and the common attributes is key to honing your flirting muscles.

Building relationships, in and out of work, requires the same skills (which I look at in the second half of this chapter), but if you've been conditioned into acting like an android rather than with your basic human instincts, you'll first need to reconnect yourself with the basic skills Mother Nature blessed us with.

This chapter deals in generalities with gender-specific behaviour, and the premises made here are based on decades of scientific and occupational research.

Looking at the Different Perceptions of Flirting

Apparently, 90 per cent of errors in thinking result from errors in perception. Whether you think someone is flirting with you or not is dependent on whether you perceive a look, comment, or action to be flirtatious in intent.

Knowing how the different sexes approach flirting can help you get ahead in the game. Being able to give clear signals that can be interpreted as the initiation of a flirtation decreases your risk of rejection because your attempts are going unnoticed and increases your chances of getting something going.

Where flirting starts and ends

Women worry about what they're going to wear and men dwell on the challenge of delivering the perfect chat-up line for good reason. Those details provide the start of the flirting spectrum for each sex.

Contrary to the animal kingdom, where often the females are dowdy and the colourful males provide the courtship displays, women are the sex generally expected to be made up attractively. Women generally feel more pressure to get their appearance right and hence put so much effort into planning and executing their look. A survey of mainly female office workers found that most of them spent over three hours planning their outfit for the Christmas party compared to less than five minutes considering lines of conversation.

Men, on the other hand, tend to believe that flirting starts the moment they open their mouth and issue a chat-up line. That's why they worry so much about what they're going to say. This opening line is also generally considered the point at which you're most at risk of rejection. As men are often the ones making the first move, they can dread this point the most.

Avoid falling into the trap of worrying about what you're going to say and reset your starting point for a flirtation to the initial eye contact. This contact is a less risky start than the 'chat-up line' approach and achieves a higher degree of success. You feel more positive about your flirting approach and create more successful outcomes.

Looking dandy

Melanie had just started dating Stuart. She'd been off the dating scene for a while and felt that perhaps she was batting out of her league, considering Stuart's trendy image. He had fashionable tousled hair and casual but chic clothes. She worried that he'd think she was a bit dowdy and made a big effort to impress him, even sneaking out of bed in the morning to apply her make-up before he woke up.

A few weeks down the line she began to realise that his wardrobe was more limited than she'd imagined. He also took himself off to the barber and returned with a conventional short haircut. She discovered that his 'up to the minute' hairstyle was by accident rather than design as he hadn't had it cut for weeks and his designer wardrobe was actually chosen for him by his mother from the retail village. When she finally confessed to him her original perceptions he could only laugh; her 'high maintenance look' had little impact on him falling for her, he was oblivious to her unwarranted fears, and he actually liked her for who she was, rather than for her attempts to be his idea of what the perfect date should be.

To be a successful flirt, you need only tailor your appearance to suit your style, not to meet your perception of somebody else's expectations.

What men and women find attractive

Opposites attract, but often for the reasons you least expect! In my flirting seminars I play a game with the attendees whereby the men say what they like and dislike when they first meet a woman and then the women do the same. I've played this game with thousands of people over the years and the results are often a surprise for each group. Here's what I find (note that this info, while not scientific, is illuminating):

- ✔ **Men:** Oddly, good looks rarely ever come up in the men's list of top ten attributes. Smile, eye contact, bottom, breasts, and legs are consistently the top of the head responses, which mirrors research on this subject. Looking and smelling good, high heels, long hair, nice nails, and being interested in them are also top answers. Having rich parents and owning a brewery have been cited as great – but not necessary – assets.

  When asked what they don't like in a woman, I'm usually met with a deafening silence in the room. Clearly, men have firm ideas about what they like but aren't too fussed about what they don't like. Facial hair, using a mobile phone during a conversation, and having a husband are top of the list of dislikes when a man first meets a woman.

What's she got that I haven't?

Karen and her friends enjoyed nothing better than a girls' night out. Recently single, she splashed out on a wardrobe of new clothes and shoes and a treasure trove of make-up. After a few weeks she was a bit disappointed at her hit rate with the men and perplexed by the success of one of her friends. She seemed to have the pick of men, even though she wasn't blessed in the looks department and her image was more 'Cheeky girls' than 'Sex and the City'.

Karen came on my Open Flirting course and applied her knowledge of the opposite sex to modifying her evening wardrobe. She ditched the black and started wearing more shapely clothes. Karen was surprised that her new image changed her 'luck' with men almost immediately, and quite horrified that grabbing a man's attention was so easy with just a tweak of the wardrobe.

When trying to impress a man, focus on what they generally like in a woman, rather than worry about what they dislike.

✔ **Women:** When first meeting the opposite sex, women noted height/stature, sense of humour, generosity, kindness, being well groomed, and half-jokingly, but consistently, having a large wallet.

Women's responses to what they didn't like in a man were spontaneous and far more extensive than the men's list. Top of the dislikes were bad breath, body odour, arrogance, joke telling, superfluous hair (nasal and ear hair and monobrows), and looking over their shoulder. Joke telling is often confused with being entertaining (see Chapter 8 on following the rules on humour for more on how to avoid this flirting gaffe).

Key to impressing a woman is avoiding the things they generally don't like in a man and emphasising the things they do.

The following sections go into a bit more detail on how you can use this information to your advantage.

Getting visual

Research shows that men are physiologically attracted. In other words, they're drawn to colour and shape, in particular colours that stand out from the crowd and the outline of the feminine form.

Wearing a demure black number makes you virtually invisible amongst every other woman with the same dress strategy. Black can cover a multitude of sins, but is a bad choice if it drops you off the radar. Colour is like a magnet; however, don't think you have to go out dressed like a parrot. Wearing colourful clothes to draw attention to your greatest assets or features is your best strategy.

Sounds great!

Kevin was the kind of guy who loved the sound of his own voice. He dominated conversations and fancied himself as a bit of a charmer. Still, after his divorce he couldn't attract a woman despite his gift of the gab.

He claimed to be very entertaining and interested in people, however an internal training seminar finally pinpointed his problem. He made all the right noises and asked questions, but never waited for an answer, and, even worse, often turned away from the person he'd just queried to start talking to someone else. He littered his conversations with jokes that people laughed politely at, whilst he smugly enjoyed his own joke-telling proficiency.

Kevin was shocked at this insight into his behaviour. He immediately started to listen to the answers to his questions and dropped the joke telling in preference to actually getting to know the people he was dealing with. He developed a genuine interest in people and the people around him responded positively; not only did he do more business, women were attracted and flattered by his interest in them.

Being interested in the people around you pays far bigger dividends than trying to be a clever conversationalist.

Next time you're at a function, or networking, scan the women in the room and see who catches your eye first. I guarantee it'll be the women wearing colourful or figure-enhancing clothes.

With the exception of 'height', women are far less specific in their desire for visual attributes. However 'height' is a bit of a misnomer; what they're actually referring to is stature. Being six foot tall but slouching along like a giant beanpole won't fit the bill. A man needs to fill his space well and hold himself with confidence. A shorter man with great posture is more attractive than a tall man with bad posture. So men, if you want to attract women, be confident and stand tall (no matter your height).

Assessing assets of the non-monetary kind

Knowing the common assets is invaluable for building any kind of relationship, not just for flirting. These assets can be used with both sexes to great effect. The top three common assets are:

- ✔ Smiling
- ✔ Maintaining eye contact
- ✔ Being interested in the other person

Desperately seeking . . .

Fran had taken a teaching post on a remote island in Scotland. Having looked forward to the opportunity, she became increasingly frustrated by her non-existent love life. The local men were thrilled at the prospect of a new woman on the island and fought fiercely for her attentions. However, Fran had a very specific picture of her Mr Perfect and none of the islanders came close. A successful city player was the profession of choice for Fran's ideal man; however, as no such institutions operated on the island, it made her idea of Mr Perfect into Mr Impossible.

When she finally put her tick list for Mr Perfect to one side, she started to see the local guys in a whole new light. Before she knew it, she was head over heals with a man she wouldn't have looked at twice in her original hunt.

High or unrealistic expectations limit your options. Discard any previous fixed ideas of what you're looking for in a person to immediately improve your flirting prospects.

Displaying the common assets with everyone you meet, both socially and professionally, gains you a reputation for being friendly and approachable, and a genuinely likeable person.

Considering Strategies for the Successful Flirt

Parting with your preconceived ideas about flirting and who Mr or Miss Right should be can give you the opportunity to expand your flirting horizons, readjust your attitudes towards flirting, and try new strategies to improve your flirting success rate. Just thinking or doing something differently can have a dramatically positive effect on your flirtatious encounters.

Looking beyond Mr or Miss Perfect

Nothing is as futile, demoralising, or limiting to your flirting agenda as having a fixed idea of how your perfect partner should be. Watching someone saving themselves exclusively for a person they've never met but who's 'fabulous looking, "x" feet tall, earns £x, has never been married, and is the life and soul of the party', is very sad. Finding Mr or Miss Goodenough is easier and more likely, especially if they too have a more forgiving list of attributes they're hoping to find in a mate.

Keeping an open mind allows you access to the biggest pool of potential flirtations. Ask your friends who're happily dating if their partners met their idea of 'perfect' when they first met them. You'll be surprised by how many people initially didn't even consider their current partner a dating option.

Keeping a list of undesirable features you wish to avoid (for example, smoking, being selfish, or wanting to see more than one person) is preferable to one of must haves when choosing people to flirt with. Just remember to keep your list short.

Rejecting the advances of someone without giving them a fair chance is a big mistake. Even if they're not your 'type', they've plucked up the courage to approach you and you should at least give them a short hearing – unless they're very drunk or objectionable!

If you give someone a fair chance and you're still not interested, keep your responses friendly rather than flirtatious so they don't get the wrong end of the stick. See Chapter 11 for more tips on handling this tricky situation. And if they still don't get the message, you can find ways to discreetly decline the advances of a clinger-on in Chapter 18.

Adopting the right flirting attitude

Flirting attitudes range from 'I can't bring myself to flirt with someone unless I know they really fancy me' to 'throw enough mud at a wall and some of it will stick'. Both attitudes present problems. At one end, you're vastly limiting your options due to fear of rejection; at the other, people who could be genuinely interested in you are put off as you may be viewed as insincere or shallow.

Moderation never killed anyone; the middle ground's the best place to start with your attitude to flirting to bag the person of your dreams.

For the reserved flirt

If your attitude towards flirting is to be very reserved, to the point of being misinterpreted as disinterested, you need to push your comfort zones to gain more success. Starting with rejection risk-free encounters, for example with people you come across in your everyday encounters, is the best approach.

If your job involves meeting people, either internally or externally, make a point of being friendly to everybody. Your confidence gets a great boost when you see the way they respond to your positive advances. If you don't work, get down to the shops and chat to the people on checkouts or become involved in a new activity.

For the flirt-with-everyone flirt

If you're very flirtatious by nature, but never seem to get the person you really want to date, don't stop being friendly, but look at what it is that makes you more flirtatious than average. Are you very charming or tactile, or do you use flirtatious body language? After you've identified how you're friendlier than average, reel it in and save it for the person you want to impress.

If the person you fancy sees you being flirtatious with everyone, they won't feel that you're treating them differently to anyone else and won't take your advances seriously.

Recognising who's available or interested

Both sexes, when choosing someone to flirt with, make the mistake of picking people that they're instantly attracted to, without first establishing if they're even interested or available.

You're attracted to what you know. If you're continually going out with the 'wrong' sort of person, the first person you find attractive probably has the same attributes. I'm not suggesting that to be a successful flirt you've got to chat up people you aren't attracted to, but establishing a basic level of interest before you pin the success of your flirtation on one person is essential. Before choosing one person to flirt with, take your time and survey the room for a number of people that you'd like to flirt with.

Overcoming fear of rejection

Rejection is both men's and women's biggest fear in relation to flirting.

Rejection itself can be crippling when it happens to you, but the *fear* of rejection is even more destructive because it can actually paralyse you into inaction. That cold, gnawing feeling in the pit of your stomach; a weakness in your limbs, a dryness in your mouth – fear feels horrible; it tests your comfort zones, and provokes a fight or flight response. The temptation to run away or say nothing when you encounter someone you find attractive or meet a colleague at work in a superior position can be overwhelming. Both genders experience this fear of rejection. Because it's generally the men who put themselves at risk of being rejected by being the ones to initiate a flirtation, however, they tend to feel more at risk.

Always maximising your chances of acceptance to minimise your chances of rejection is the trick to overcoming this fear. Having a positive attitude also helps enormously with your success rate. Head to Chapter 15 for advice that can help you never again worry about being rejected.

Making flirting easy to spot

The key to starting a flirtation is making it easy to spot. Make sure that the person you want to flirt with can see that your behaviour with them is different to the behaviour you demonstrate to the other people around them. Chapter 10 covers how to give off the right signals.

Some people need more evidence that a flirtation is on offer than others before they'll reciprocate. For example, when making eye contact, look at them for longer than you would look at other people in the room, smile more at them than at the other people around you, have a smaller proximity between you than with others, and so on. This way it's obvious to the person that you're treating them differently and if the feeling is mutual they'll reciprocate.

You're much more likely to initiate a fabulous flirtation if you're dressed for the part. Chapter 5 offers plenty of makeover ideas. Dressing for success makes you feel more confident and is much more likely to bring you flirting success.

Don't play it cool. It can be misinterpreted as disinterest.

Using flattery

Whoever said flattery gets you nowhere certainly wasn't referring to flirting. Flattering them is a key technique for letting the other person know you're interested in them or find them attractive.

Paying genuine compliments is essential if they're to be received well. If you dish out the same stock compliment to everyone, the person you're complimenting won't feel very special when they realise. Compliments needn't be limited to someone's appearance; they can relate to their personality or something they've done. Chapter 9 offers lots of ideas on using compliments.

Practise paying compliments daily, to friends, relatives, and colleagues, to master the art of delivering them with ease.

Backfiring compliments

I was running a seminar for a large bank recently and in the break was inundated with questions from the delegates. Most people joined in the conversation, but I could see a guy out of the corner of my eye loitering on the periphery. Eventually he pushed into the group, sidled up, and complimented me on having great shoes. I'm a huge shoe fan, and was flattered by his compliment and thanked him for it. Unfortunately, he followed it up with, 'When's Halloween, then?' referring, I assume, to their pointy-ness. I was mortified that he would insult my lovely shoes in such a juvenile way. 'Flattery will get you nowhere,' I responded, as I turned my back on him and effectively cut him out of the group.

Only ever pay genuine compliments, and never joke about one with someone you don't know, because they're unlikely to be amused by it and may even be offended.

Chapter 4

Flirting with Friends, Dates, and Colleagues

● ●

In This Chapter

▶ Flirting among friends

▶ Being more than friends

▶ Dating intentions

▶ Flirting at work

● ●

As a rule, flirting not only makes you feel good, it makes the people around you feel really special, too. Italians, for example, flirt with everyone, from their friends to their partner to their grandmother. They have an energy, passion, and enthusiasm for life and for people that's refreshing to be around.

You can flirt with anyone: friends, colleagues, and strangers you want to get to know. But how do you go about flirting with friends and colleagues without making existing relationships feel awkward? And how do you judge whether strangers you're interested in are open to flirtatious overtures? This chapter gives the details.

Flirting with Friends

Flirting with friends is a natural and enjoyable behaviour. Two types of flirting with friends exist:

✔ *Platonic flirting* – the innocent mutual type with both male and female friends. This type of flirting happens naturally when you're enjoying each other's company.

✔ Flirting with romantic intent – with a friend you're attracted to or vice versa.

Being just good friends

George met Cleo at a conference overseas. They got to know each other well over the course of a few days and were quite inseparable. Both were married and had children and they shared similar values. Much to George and Cleo's amusement, many delegates commented that they made an attractive couple. In reality, however outrageously they appeared to flirt with each other, there was no intention on either part for it to be anything more than friendly. A certain security existed in the fact that they were both happy in their respective relationships, and by hanging out together they were safe from the advances of delegates with less honourable intentions.

Flirting harmlessly with married people is perfectly acceptable provided the feelings and intent are mutual.

Flirting with friends paves the way for developing positive relationships, making new friends, and potentially moving the relationship beyond friendship to romance. This kind of flirting can continue to flourish trouble free to everyone's benefit, provided the feeling is mutual and everyone knows the limitations of the flirtation. The following sections explain how to get the basics right.

Friendly flirting

Friendly flirting consists of smiling, making good eye contact, and showing interest in other people – the common assets for both sexes mentioned in Chapter 3. This type of flirting is suitable for both sexes and all ages.

Telling if someone is just being friendly is relatively straightforward. If they're demonstrating only the common behaviours listed in the preceding paragraph, you can assume that the flirtation is purely friendly.

Adopt friendly flirting as your general approach to everyone. This type of flirting prepares your flirting skills for the more advanced flirting techniques when you want to bag a date. And, you never know who's watching you: your friendly behaviour could be just the cue they need to have the confidence to approach you.

Flirting with intent: The signs

Flirting with intent is when someone's interested in being more than just friends and their behaviour changes to indicate the romantic motive behind their actions. This intention is hormone-fuelled, and being able to tell when this is happening is useful for either progressing a relationship or avoiding leading that person on.

Establishing if someone wants more than friendship is useful when you're flirting with intent or are trying to determine whether someone else is flirting with intent with you.

People who flirt with intent do more than simply smile, make good eye contact, and show an interest. Watch for these behaviours:

- ✔ Standing close to you
- ✔ Touching you more than they touch other people
- ✔ Preening themselves more than usual, perhaps by fixing their hair or smoothing their clothes, and so on
- ✔ Making longer eye contact with you than with other people
- ✔ Paying more compliments to you than is usual for them
- ✔ Making more of an effort with their appearance when with you, perhaps by choosing more impressive outfits to wear

Research has shown that men can tend to interpret signs of friendliness as signs of sexual availability. Checking for the behaviours in this list (or, in other words, deciding whether she is demonstrating more than just smiling, good eye contact, and an interest in you) is a prudent move to make.

These behaviours are also different to their behaviour towards the other people around you. See Chapter 12 for more on how to read flirting signals.

People who like or are in tune with you mirror your body language. *Mirroring* is simply where we copy the other person's gestures, body language, or behaviour. For example, if the other person crosses their leg towards you, and you mirror them, you cross your leg towards them. If you're curious whether the person with whom you're flirting with intent feels the same way about you, watch to see if they mirror your actions or respond favourably.

Moving from 'just friends'

Being considered someone's friend is always an honour and a privilege. Not only is friendship good for the soul, it bestows considerable health benefits, too. Some of your best memories and most cherished moments involve friends. Your friends may also provide a delicately balanced system for nurturing each other. These are the benefits you have to weigh up when considering risking converting a friend to a lover.

Sweet as Candy

Candy had a huge crush on a colleague. They'd enjoy friendly banter in the office, but she never got the feeling it was anything more than an innocent flirtation, the same as he enjoyed with the other girls in the office. However, she didn't see that the feeling of attraction was mutual. He actually fancied her as much as she secretly lusted after him. Unfortunately this mutual attraction was masked as they mirrored each other's body language. If she caught him looking at her, she'd look away; when she looked away, he'd be worried that he'd embarrassed her and would look away too, so when she looked back, he wasn't looking and she'd get the impression that he wasn't interested. Once Candy got over her initial shyness about flirting properly with him, the signals were clear for them both to see.

Make your body language explicit to give the person you're assessing a proper chance to react.

Think carefully whether you're prepared to risk your current relationship *before* you embark on a route that may well be one-way only. Re-establishing your old relationship can be incredibly difficult.

The following sections offer advice to help you navigate the move from the role of friend to something more.

Avoid sending mixed signals

Avoiding mixed messages is vital when you've taken the plunge of moving on from the role of friend. When you've committed to your new way of behaving, don't deviate and your romantic flirtation will flourish. Things to consider include:

- ✔ **If you're starting to behave as though you're initiating a romantic flirtation, you have to dress and look the part.** Ladies, if you don't normally wear much make-up when you're with him, start wearing more, or wear it differently so he'll notice. Men, up the grooming and invest in an aftershave you've not worn before. Getting her to choose it with you guarantees that she'll like it! Go to Chapter 5 for more information.

- ✔ **If you've been turning up the heat in terms of your body language and you're getting a positive reaction, you have to let your friend see that you're making an effort with your appearance, too.** Turning up dressed in your dog-walking outfit when going out for a drink confuses the situation.

Happy campers

University friends, Harry and Jane, went to work on Harry's aunt's farm for the summer holidays. Harry had always fancied Jane and saw this job as an ideal opportunity to get her to himself. They lived in a happy little commune with lots of international students and everyone mucked in with the chores.

Housemates kept enquiring as to the nature of their relationship. 'Just friends,' replied Jane. Secretly, Jane suspected that Harry's feelings towards her were more than friendly, but she ignored them and positioned the relationship as a purely platonic friendship.

Eventually, Harry's unsubtle hints gave way to a full-blown admission of being head over heels in love with her. He issued Jane an ultimatum – lovers or nothing. Unfortunately for Harry, she chose nothing. She valued Harry as a friend but had never given him any indication that she wanted anything more. The atmosphere in the house was tense until the matter blew over and Jane reconciled Harry to being 'just friends'.

If your attempts to move a relationship to a new level are ignored, declaring undying love is unlikely to give you the result you hoped for.

✔ **If you socialise in a group, your behaviour towards your potential date in group settings also has to change.** Suddenly reverting to treating them the way you always have (for example, by sitting at a distance and speaking to other people more) confuses them. Keep a closer proximity and use more smiles, eye contact, and touching for them than for the rest of the group.

Dithering on the border between friendly and romantic flirtation is confusing for everyone – friends and the object of your desire alike.

Don't become a friend just to become something more

Making the mistake of becoming somebody's friend in order to get closer to them can align you to the category of 'just friends' – a difficult trap to escape from whilst preserving the relationship.

If you're embarking on a flirtation with somebody new, approaching the situation romantically is much more effective than endearing yourself to them as a friend and then trying to make the switch. When you take the trusted position of a shoulder to cry on, particularly when it comes to an ex, it can be difficult for your 'friend' to see you as a romantic prospect.

If you're becoming a shoulder to cry on, deflect your friend onto someone else by saying, 'That's awful for you; I do empathise but I think X would be a much better person to speak to about it. Let *me* take you out for a drink to cheer you up.'

 Most people refer to their relationship with a friend as simply 'friends'. When someone has to justify the relationship as 'just friends', it usually means some unqualified suspicion exists that one or both parties consider the relationship as something more.

Flirting with Dates

Starting a flirtation with a potential date is different to flirting with friends. You have to start with a much stronger approach because you get less opportunity to form a first impression with a potential date than with a friend, and you need to make your intentions absolutely clear.

Flirtation's best bit is the chase. If you're not used to reading the signs and find the chase traumatic, you'll soon come to enjoy it after you've learnt to give off and interpret all the right signals. Chapter 11 offers lots of tips on how to read body language before you get going.

Making your intentions clear

Showing your intentions would be child's play if you could simply wear a badge displaying them. Wearing 'You're lovely, am I your type?' on your chest would save a lot of 'do they, don't they fancy me' analysis, but wouldn't be half the fun.

You can show your intentions by doing things like dressing to impress, smelling great, looking confident, giving them your full undivided attention with great levels of eye contact, showing plenty of smiles, mirroring their body language, and touching intentionally. (See Chapter 11 for more info about body language.)

 Decide how fast you're prepared to take things and prepare to act accordingly. If you want to get to know someone gradually, pressing for a late night invitation back to their place is probably going to get you more than an offer of coffee. Alternatively, spending months being polite and waiting for an invitation to hold hands may also lead to a degree of frustration on both sides.

Commuter code

Penny had seen Mike on the Tube several days a week for the last three weeks. He had a slightly aloof look about him and usually buried his nose in the paper during his journey. They both got off at the same stop, but she hadn't managed to catch his attention to make a move and clearly she was invisible to him. Not wanting to miss her opportunity and keen to see if Mike was actually spoken for, Penny took decisive action. The next day, having dolled herself up, she positioned herself so that she faced him, and stared at his paper. When he dropped it to turn the page, he saw her staring at him. She looked away, then back again; he was still looking at her – he was interested! She looked away again and he carried on with his newspaper.

The next time he caught her eye when turning a page, she gave him a coy smile and in response he sat up straight and smiled back. She looked away again and he returned to his paper. The next time he dropped his paper, she could see him checking if she was looking, so she poked her tongue out. He laughed in surprise. As Penny left the train, she looked over her shoulder to see Mike catching up with her and she gave him a big grin and a cheery hello. They went out for a drink that night before taking the Tube home together.

By being obvious in her intentions, not only did Penny get noticed, her confidence impressed Mike enough to ask her out without worrying if he was making a move that wouldn't be reciprocated. Being brave in your actions will be rewarded.

Interpreting reactions and intentions

In days of yore, you'd be issued with a letter of intent or contract for marriage when someone had honourable intentions towards you; a bit formal, perhaps, but it removed the possibility of misinterpretation and missed opportunities. Now you want to interpret the other person's intentions. Unfortunately, your interpretation of someone's intentions isn't always accurate.

Being able to interpret reactions and intentions requires good observational skills on your part. Pay attention to the following:

- Do they behave in the same manner with you when you're on your own as they do when you're with others?
- If you're off colour, are they concerned?
- If your mood alters, does their mood alter accordingly?
- Are they adopting your language cues, using phrases and terms peculiar to you?
- What does their body language say? (Remember to look for these clues in clusters of four or more. Chapter 11 has more on body language.)

Lucky pants

Derek had been flirting gently with Sally for months in their local bars and clubs, but had never managed to move things on. Sally was waiting for a definitive flirtation, aimed directly at her and without the confusion of not being able to tell if he was just being friendly or if he really fancied her. One Saturday night they must both have been in the same frame of mind. Sally applied her war paint immaculately, squeezed into her pulling dress and sprayed herself liberally with the perfume that made her feel at her sexiest. Derek put on his lucky pants, splashed on some after-shave that his sister swore would make any woman weak, and headed into town.

When Derek saw Sally, he congratulated himself on his decision to wear the lucky pants, as she was a picture and he intended to score. She fixed him with a look and he ignored all the other women he would normally speak to and made a beeline for her. Derek and Sally finally got it together thanks to a decisive bit of action on both their parts.

Whether your lucky pants set your mind to it or your favourite perfume, use something as the catalyst to keep you focused on displaying and following up your intentions.

 Get used to looking for clusters of clues; they're vital to reading, interpreting, and reacting to friends and flirtations alike. Never base your decision on any one gesture in isolation. You almost need a library of reactions to different situations to build up a picture of a person's intentions.

Flirting with Colleagues

Most of us find our partner in the workplace. Whilst most companies shudder at the potential litigation prospects of a failed office romance, little can be done to stop them happening.

 Although you may think you're being discreet, employers have ways of 'finding' things out, even if they're not actively looking.

Flirting with unemployment: Sexual harassment

Make sure you're fully aware of the legal position before you start in hot pursuit of your colleague. Avoiding accusations of *sexual harassment* – unwelcome and uninvited physical, verbal, or visual behaviour that is sexual in nature – is crucial but fraught with ambiguity.

One man's compliment is another woman's harassment

Richard could've been described as the office creep. The older women were used to him creeping up and complimenting them over their shoulders. Although they found this behaviour unnerving, Richard was essentially harmless and had never actually done anything more inappropriate to anyone.

When Richard tried to make an impression on the new girl in the office, however, she took an instant dislike to him and found his approach offensive. She accused him of sexual harassment and reported him to human resources. Richard was flabbergasted and protested he didn't mean anything by his actions; indeed, he'd behaved this way with the other women in the office for years. Human resources pointed out to him that intention is irrelevant; how the recipient perceives his behaviour is what defines sexual harassment. Luckily, Richard walked away with a warning and managed to keep his job.

Following are important things to know:

- ✔ **Sexual harassment refers to how the recipient interpreted an action, *not* how it was intended by the offender.** For example, a man may think he's being friendly paying a woman in the office a compliment. However, if she's offended by his action then it can be considered sexual harassment, even if other women in the office aren't offended by the same man paying them compliments. Or if a woman insists on touching colleagues or kissing people on greeting and a man finds this invasive or offensive, this too can be interpreted as sexual harassment.

- ✔ **Ignorance is no defence in the eyes of the law.** Many companies send their employees on sexual harassment courses; first, to educate staff on how to avoid it, and, second, to indemnify them against liability if someone who has been educated on the matter does actually commit a sexual harassment offence.

- ✔ **Sexual harassment can be a career-limiting event.** A sexual harassment conviction usually puts you straight to the top of the reject pile in the short-listing process.

Flirting boundaries at work

Flirting at work involves a slightly different strategy to flirting in a bar. Whereas in a bar you initially assess *all* the people you find attractive to see if they're interested and available, that sort of approach in the workplace earns you a poor reputation and may even put off Mr or Miss Right.

You can take two approaches:

- ✔ Letting people know you're available.
- ✔ Being generally more friendly.

A combination of both approaches is very effective for grabbing attention in the office and turning the right heads.

Letting people know you're available

Generally, nothing goes unnoticed at work. It may not be mentioned, but certainly everything's been observed. Alter your wardrobe, hairstyle, make-up, glasses, your posture, and even the way you initiate and conduct conversations and people will notice a change in you. A makeover attracts the attention of your colleagues and possibly gains the interest of people you didn't even realise were aware of you – taking a lot of leg work out of the flirting process. (Chapter 5 has tips and advice for how to give yourself a DIY flirting makeover.)

Being more friendly

Being friendlier is a great strategy for every aspect of your life. Smiling and making more eye contact are the keys to appearing more friendly. Behaviour breeds behaviour and people who like you mirror your friendly actions. Adopting a friendly approach is a great way to attract a flirtation and to pick up more friends generally, especially as you age. Opportunities to make more friends decrease the older you get.

Head turner

Claire had finished with her boyfriend and decided to advertise the fact with a radical makeover. She dyed her hair a gorgeous chestnut brown, which was fabulous, but sadly not on her. Everybody in the office noticed the change for the worse but said nothing. Eventually one of her friends had a quiet word and took her to her hairstylist. Claire returned a stunning redhead.

Gary had noticed both changes, but only ventured forth to comment after the second makeover. They began a very tentative and discreet flirtation in the office, which endured for some time before they were sure that an office romance was something they both wanted.

You can attract as well as initiate flirting at work by making bold statements that don't actually involve saying anything.

Help the aged

Jess and Ian had been discreetly flirting at work. They wanted to flirt more but not in the office. They didn't have many company functions, except the obligatory Christmas party and that was months away.

Jess's gran hadn't been well and Help the Aged had provided wonderful support for her. Jess saw an opportunity to spend more time with Ian and do something for her gran's charity. She organised a fund-raising 24-hour bike ride, involving people from work and their friends. Preparation meant a gruelling schedule of training events and seeing lots of Ian outside work. Not only did running this event improve her organisational skills, Jess also lost weight, made lots of new friends, and she and Ian were free to flirt outrageously on neutral ground.

If no events take place at work, organise one of your own!

People are much more likely to like you if they think you like them.

Taking flirting outside work

Flirting in the workplace is fine if you're discreet. If you're involved in a full-on flirtation, using overt sexual gesturing, the office isn't the place. Similarly, if you feel uncomfortable, or suspect the other person would feel more comfortable continuing the flirtation without the obtrusive interest of your colleagues, take it outside the workplace. You may not feel ready to ask them for a date, so picking an event when you can continue your flirtation in more appropriate circumstances is key to ramping up your flirtation. Most workplaces have social gatherings, informal events, or get-togethers. Some people dread these functions, but, like the lottery, you have to be in it to win it.

If no events are planned, get yourself involved in workplace committees and propose an event yourself. If you're self-employed or not in paid work, joining an organisation that matches your interests is also a good way to find flirting opportunities.

Part II
Getting Noticed! Making Contact

The 5th Wave   By Rich Tennant

"Stop flirting already and ask him to throw us a line!"

In this part . . .

I help you catapult yourself into the flirting limelight by oozing confidence, turning heads with your film star entrance, and making great conversation with absolutely everybody and anybody.

Chapter 5

Boosting Self-Confidence and Giving Yourself a Flirting Makeover

In This Chapter

▶ Creating your personalised makeover

▶ Achieving a confident look

▶ Sounding the part

C onfidence is attractive, sexy, and supercharges your pulling power. Being confident is a game of two halves: inner confidence – which nobody can see or feel other than you – and outer confidence – which is the level of confidence that is perceived by the people around you. In an ideal world, quickly fixing your inner confidence would be great. Doing so, however, can be time consuming and is actually unnecessary because only your 'outer' perceived confidence needs to be up to scratch. This chapter gives you all the pointers you need to present a confident demeanour.

 Very often, when we improve our outer confidence we're so taken by the results of our efforts that our inner confidence gets a boost, which makes us outwardly more confident, and, before you know it, this circular process has magical effects on both inner and outer confidence. So when it comes to confidence, fake it till you make it.

The DIY Flirting Makeover: Getting Started

Changing your look catches people's attention. Changing it to something that is appropriate for your personality, circumstances, and the style you wish to convey can be a massive boost to your confidence in itself. Updating a look that you've outgrown can knock years off you, and attracts the sort of people you want to appeal to.

The bulk of this chapter explains the various ways you can change your appearance, demeanour, and outlook to both build and project an aura of confidence. The following sections outline how to decide what type of image or style you want to adopt and tell you how to prioritise the changes you decide to make.

Creating the image you want to project

Working with many image consultants, I note that they're united in their opinion that knowing what image you want to project is vital in creating the right image for you. If you want to be perceived as a sex kitten, then wearing a dull polo neck jumper and old leggings isn't going to help you achieve the look. Or if you want to impress the ladies with an air of sophistication but your favourite outfit is your tracksuit, you'll be disappointed with your results.

No right or wrong style exists. Different shapes, colours, styles, and textures work better for one body shape than for another. Determine your shape and style and dress to suit them and the image you wish to project. For expert advice you can:

- ✔ Consult books by the TV makeover gurus.

- ✔ See an image or branding consultant. Visit www.colourme beautiful.co.uk or www.tfic.org.uk.

- ✔ Visit a personal shopper in a department store. Debenhams provides this service for free; others may charge.

Choosing the areas to focus on

Looking at the different aspects of your image and applying the 80:20 rule – using 20 per cent of your effort to improve 80 per cent of your appearance (refer to Chapter 2) – you'll be able to determine the changes that will give you the most impact the quickest. If you haven't thought about your image in a while, ask a few friends to do it with you. They may see you in a different light.

Use Table 5-1, which lists ten areas of improvement, to determine what area can yield the most significant results. Follow these steps:

1. In the first column, give each item a score from 1 to 10, with 1 signifying the easiest/quickest to change and 10 the hardest/slowest.

   Use each number only once.

2. In the second column, do the same, with 1 representing the most significant in improving your makeover and 10 the least significant.

3. In the third column, multiply the two rows together.

4. Pick the two areas with the lowest scores.

   These indicate what two items are the quickest to achieve with the biggest impact on your overall image.

5. When you've cracked the two items in point 4, carry on working your way through the list to the highest numbers until you've completed your overhaul.

Table 5-1	Image Assessment Tool		
Area of Improvement	*Ease/Speed of Improvement*	*Importance of Improvement to Makeover*	*Multiply First Column by Second Column*
Hair			
Make-up			
Skin			
Eyes			
Smile			
Work wardrobe			
Social wardrobe			
Shoes			
Voice			
Perfume			

The remaining sections in this chapter offer advice on making improvements in these areas.

Shopping bonus

Louise was in her thirties. She was carrying more weight than she had in her twenties and it wouldn't budge. Following promotion, she didn't feel her look matched her new shape or job. She'd always worn tightish clothes with shortish hemlines but now felt they undermined her credibility and made her look slightly ridiculous. She didn't know what style to aim for, so took herself off to a personal shopper for some advice.

Waiting to see the shopper, Louise caught the eye of Mark, who was also about to have a style makeover. He was dressing too young for his age and found himself the butt of his kids' jokes, but he didn't know how to dress appropriately without looking old. They made polite conversation as they waited, both aware of the reason for their visit, but neither mentioning it. A few hours later, Louise and Mark emerged, clutching their new purchases and sporting a new look and air of confidence. Louise complimented Mark on his new appearance and he reciprocated. He asked her to join him for coffee, an invitation she wouldn't normally have accepted, which ran into dinner and they dated happily ever after.

Making small changes can create big results and give you the confidence to behave differently and take more risks.

Looking Ten Years Younger

Unless you're 21, like most people you wouldn't object to looking younger. A youthful appearance is highly valued in our culture; women with the physique, style, and energy of a woman of Madonna's age didn't exist a few years ago, but are commonplace now. More men than ever are having cosmetic surgery and enhancement, and from an earlier age, and grooming and anti-ageing products fly off the shelves in unprecedented volumes. Having a lived-in face is no longer an indication of gaining wisdom with age; unfortunately, wrinkles and grey hair are seen as indications of being too lazy to care for your appearance.

 Prevention is better than cure when it comes to ageing. Don't smoke, drink alcohol in moderation and water in abundance, sleep well, and use a moisturiser with a minimum Sun Protection Factor (SPF) of 15 to remain younger looking for longer.

To look younger, you need to address the key areas of your eyes, teeth, skin, hair colour and style, and clothing.

Down in the mouth

Alice was a widow in her sixties. She'd always hated her teeth and as a result never smiled. People often mistakenly thought she was miserable, but that couldn't be farther from the truth.

When she unexpectedly came into some money, Alice decided to have her teeth straightened with braces. Eighteen months later, the braces were removed and, for maximum effect, Alice also had her teeth whitened. The result was astounding. Alice finally had the confidence to smile freely, and she wished she'd done it years ago. People now react to the smiley Alice in a completely different way and she feels much more positive about herself, too.

Don't put off changing something because you think you've left it too late. Making yourself feel good by investing in your appearance is always worthwhile.

Eyes

People make their first contact with another person with their eyes. The eyes let the other person see how interested we are in them and play a vital part in communication.

When giving your eyes a makeover, pay particular attention to these areas:

- **Brows:** Your brows frame your eyes; regardless of gender, they need to be well maintained and shaped. (Men are no strangers to having their brows seen to these days, especially where monobrows – a single eyebrow that stretches from one eye to the other across the bridge of the nose – are concerned.) Right and left brows don't need to be identical; think of them more as siblings. Get them shaped by a beautician and then you can pluck the stragglers yourself.

  Never shave excess hairs from the brow: the regrowth looks terrible. Always wax or pluck.

- **Black bags:** Black bags under the eyes are terribly ageing. A concealer covers very dark circles and a light-reflecting concealer bounces back the light off you and makes your eyes look much younger. Use an eye cream or gel for dark circles; the gentle massaging effect when applying it also helps drain excess fluid from the area.

✔ **Wrinkles:** Treat wrinkles with an anti-wrinkle cream to plump out the skin and reduce their appearance. Eye creams and gels are available at prices ranging from £6 to over £100. Because the correct application can have as much effect as the product itself, don't worry that you have to spend a fortune. Go to a beauty counter and ask for a demonstration on applying eye cream and a recommendation for a product for your eyes.

 Don't use moisturiser in the delicate eye area; the cream's too heavy and can make your skin puffy. Also try to avoid rubbing the delicate eye area; use a gentle patting motion instead.

 If the white of your eyes isn't bright white, lay off the booze and watch it brighten up. If your eyes are dry from travelling or from too much VDU use, try using over-the-counter eye drops.

Smile

Ten years ago, nobody cared about the colour of your teeth, but now darker teeth are seen as very ageing. Make sure, at the very least, that your teeth are clean by visiting the hygienist every six months, and keep that cleanliness topped up with a whitening toothpaste. A bright smile is very youthful. For professionally whitened teeth, avoid using a beautician and go to the dentist for a professional, longer-lasting result.

 Use a lip salve with a good Sun Protection Factor (SPF) to keep your lips soft, plump, and kissable. To keep them extra luscious, exfoliate your lips once a week with a dab of Vaseline and a gentle rub with a toothbrush.

Skin

Drinking lots of water, exfoliating once a week, using an age-appropriate moisturiser, and avoiding prolonged amounts of sunbathing are the biggest favours you can do your skin. Although sunlight has positive effects on your mood and contains vital vitamin D, it does terrible damage to the skin, so cover up when you're out in it. Consider splashing out on a beauty counter product instead of a supermarket special; the exfoliating grains are much finer and the results more impressive. Fortunately, exfoliating creams aren't that expensive nowadays and you can get a good one for between £10 and £20, which will last for ages.

Head turner

Anne had managed to get herself an appointment with one of the most sought-after hairstylists in town. She took her sister, Paula, with her and warned her that whatever her hair looked like she had to say it was fantastic. After a considerable wait, Anne emerged resembling Rod Stewart's long lost brother. Paula started to gush about how wonderful she looked, as instructed. Anne hissed at her to be quiet and dragged her out of the salon. After suffering a week of ridicule, Anne sought a recommendation for a hairdresser who would style her hair according to what suited her rather than simply follow the latest trend. The next cut suited her to a tee thanks to a stylist who had a reputation for making people look good.

When going for a radical change, make sure you pick a stylist that gives you what you want, not what they want.

Nowadays, several skin-care products are marketed specifically for men. Often, the marketing is the only difference between the male and female versions, as the products themselves are actually the same, particularly with eye gels and other non-scented products. So men, you can try borrowing your female friends' and relatives' products to see what you like before investing. Women, the male products are sometimes cheaper. Ask discreetly before you buy the ladies' version.

Hair

Hair has always been considered a person's crowning glory. Great-looking hair is a sign of vitality, fertility, and health – several of the key things we look for at a primal level when selecting a mate. Poor hair can be a confidence crusher, but with today's products, even hair loss sufferers can improve the appearance of what's left and so increase their confidence.

If you're lucky enough to have a fabulous head of hair to frame your face, use it to your advantage. Preening is one of the key flirting signals. Avoid clogging your hair up with products and wear it in a loose style so that you can play with it around the object of your desires. Playing with your hair draws attention to your face and keeps a person looking at your eyes and mouth, thus making them aware of the flirting signals you're projecting.

Colour

Colouring your hair is a great way to boost your confidence, but be careful as you get older because your skin tone fades and can't take the strength of your original hair colour. When you get into your late thirties, or if you've started to go grey, always choose a lighter colour than your original shade. Go for the best colour treatment you can afford. Be clear about what you want and be open to taking advice from professionals. Ask for recommendations. If you're colouring your grey hair yourself, make sure to pick a product that is specifically designed to do so; if you choose something with 'warm' in the title, for example 'warm chestnut', it contains red, which eventually fades to leave you with pinky grey hair.

Men's hair-colouring products are often cheaper than the female equivalent.

Volume

Fine, limp, or thin hair can be transformed with volumising shampoos and styling products. Wash regularly with a cool rinse after a warm shampoo to create a glossy finish – making clean hair look more voluminous is easier and dirty hair emphasises thinness. Blow dry hair upside down to boost root volume and finish with a good hairspray.

Quantity

Experiencing thinning hair and baldness is on the increase in both sexes (over 30 per cent of women will suffer). Trichologists (medical specialists who deal with the hair and scalp) agree that prevention is better than cure. Keeping thinning hair is easier than trying to grow it back after you're bald.

You can sometimes prevent and/or correct non-hereditary hair loss by adopting a good protein and mineral-rich diet, which also improves your hair's appearance. If your hair loss is hereditary, you can use minoxodil-based products (available on the high street or from trichologists), which are effective in preventing further loss and can often reverse the process.

Hair salons aren't the place to go for advice; they're generally only aware of thickening products and aren't medically qualified. For advice on your particular problem, visit www.trichologists.org.uk.

Also consider taking a look at www.nanogen.co.uk, from which you can purchase nanofibres. *Nanofibres* are tiny fibres that bind together electrostatically over a thinning or bald patch to cosmetically cover the area, and make an enormously effective cosmetic fix for disguising thinning hair. These nanofibres are rain- and sweatproof, so when you've fixed them with the fixing spray you can be confident that they'll stay bonded to the hair, and you can simply wash them out afterwards. If you need a temporary fix (for example, in the case of women after childbirth suffering from temporary hair loss) nanofibres can be a great confidence boost. Many people use this method on a daily basis, but the fix is only cosmetic and just disguises the problem without curing it.

Scent

Smell is the only sense that is processed directly by the brain, which makes it incredibly powerful. Smell is an evocative sense; consider smelling fresh coffee, baking bread, cut grass, hospitals, or bad breath – they all tend to evoke strong positive or negative feelings. Wearing a seductive scent can make you irresistible and body odour can make you equally as repulsive.

Using one perfume or aftershave for all occasions loses its potency. Try building a 'fragrance wardrobe' so that you have a range of different scents to meet your different moods. Avoid cheap fragrances, but if you can't afford expensive perfumes, aim to smell fresh and clean. Remember to try before you buy to avoid wasting money and be aware that all fragrances don't smell the same on one person as they do on another because of the chemical differences in our skin.

Key to making a scent work for you is associating it with a memory. When you're feeling really sexy, wear your sexy perfume or aftershave. The next time you smell it, you'll associate it with the feeling of being really sexy and you'll be straight back in that mood. Scent has the added bonus of affecting the memory of the person you're flirting with, too, so pick perfume or aftershave that is particular to you and not just the latest bestseller.

When buying perfumes or aftershaves, never try more than a few at a time because your nose will be overwhelmed. Also spray them onto a paper strip so you don't get overwhelmed by too much fragrance on your body.

Clothes

Being comfortable in your clothes, in the way they fit and their appropriateness for the occasion, is key to being able to wear them well and oozing confidence as you do so:

- ✔ **Fit, style, and colours of clothes:** If you don't want to be overlooked when out socialising, don't wear cheap, badly fitting, or dowdy-coloured clothes (see Figures 5-1 and 5-2). Better to invest in a few good pieces than buying a lot of cheap clothes.

- ✔ **Appropriateness of clothes:** If you want to be noticed when you're socialising, buy clothes that impress and stand out for the right reasons in your social environment. For example, heels on a woman not only give stature, they give shapely legs, too. Go for what looks good on your body shape and that suits your style. Determine the image you want to create and dress the part.

Dress for the job you want, not the one you have. Likewise, dress for the person you want to attract.

Figure 5-1: Inappropriate dress for social occasions.

Figure 5-2: Serious flirting wear for social occasions.

Getting the right fit

Men who wear their trousers too tight either haul them down under their stomach or hoick them up under their armpits. Neither is a good look. Biting the bullet and buying a bigger size until you lose the extra pounds is far better.

Women who are uncomfortable wearing tight or short outfits spend the whole time clawing at them to try and achieve better coverage. If tight or short isn't for you, then wear something you're more comfortable in or strap yourself up with some serious control underwear.

Shop for clothes with a trusted advisor who tells you the truth about what looks good and what doesn't. Many shop assistants will sell you anything to make the sale, but not only do you want your clothes to fit you properly, you want them to enhance your shape and style. You want your clothes to represent yourself at your best.

Accessorising

The little things can often make a big difference. Accessorise your outfit with items that are personal to you and reflect your personality. You feel more interesting showing a little bit of yourself and give people an opportunity to compliment you, building rapport and your confidence. Accessorising is easier for women because a much larger range of accessories exists. Avoid too much jewellery, guys, unless you're trying to achieve the Peter Stringfellow look!

Men, pick unusual or very high quality accessories, from watches and scarves to shoes and ties, to give yourself a confident self-assured air. Also, the type of shirt collar, the style of knot, and the choice of pattern is a way of accessorising to suit you.

Looking and Sounding Confident

Looking confident is half the battle, even if you don't feel it. Creating the appearance of confidence is a very powerful flirting tool. To do this, think back to a time when you felt supremely confident and work out what it was about that situation that made you feel so good about yourself. It was probably a combination of the way you looked and felt. Remembering all those great feelings and sensations can help inspire you to boost your confidence on a daily basis and in difficult situations. Drawing on that experience and convincing yourself that you can look and feel confident is a great skill.

Adopting a confident posture is a great outward sign of confidence, and pulling yourself up to your full height, keeping your eyes front and your head high, gives you an instant confidence makeover. When people react to you positively, it boosts your confidence from the inside and the confidence-cranking process begins.

People like to be around confident people because it inspires confidence in them. You're much more likely to want to mix, flirt, or work with people you have confidence in, and more likely to trust people who look confident. With increased confidence comes more friends, and greater professional success and satisfaction, too.

A fine line exists between confidence and arrogance, which you have to be careful not to cross. Being bullish is more likely to alienate people and turn them off. At the opposite end of the spectrum, lack of confidence and assertiveness can lead not only to a lack of faith in you but also in your abilities.

Confident people are prepared to take risks whereas arrogant people often avoid risk taking, or if they do take risks they are quick to place the blame on others for their failure. Confident people bounce back from failures and can keep them in perspective. They don't let one bad thing ruin an otherwise positive day.

Overcoming confidence killers

Quashing your own confidence is a bad habit to slip into and most of us inadvertently do it from time to time. Identifying the problem and stopping it reverses the process and your confidence bounces back to top form in no time.

Two sources of confidence killer exist:

- ✔ **You:** When someone pays you a compliment, do you accept it or blush, ignore it, or play it down? Accept it, is the right answer; any other response either shows a lack of compliment etiquette (see Chapter 9) or a willingness to knock your own confidence. When listening to your conversations, do you notice that you add negative comments about yourself at the end of sentences, such as 'stupid me', 'well, that would happen to me', and 'I'm useless'? If so, get a friend to stop you mid-conversation whenever you're being negative to break the habit of putting yourself down.

- ✔ **The people around you:** Do you have a friend, relative, or colleague who has little digs at you, even in jest? Your subconscious doesn't have a sense of humour, so it processes them all as fact and gradually persuades you that you are as stupid and useless as they tell you. Negative people are emotional vampires; they suck the vitality and confidence out of you. Staying away from them or persuading them to modify their language and behaviour to be more positive are the only ways to deal with these people. If the person in question happens to be your best friend, then perhaps you need to put your friendly flirting skills to good use and find a new one. Unlike puppies, best friends don't have to be for life.

Not-so-lucky Lucy

Lucy had just started at a new school. Unfortunately, the boy she sat next to made snide comments whenever she answered a question wrongly and constantly told her to put her hand down in class as she wouldn't know the answer. His poisonous attitude gradually crushed Lucy's confidence. Following a word with the teacher by her parents, the boy was moved. Apparently, he was actually a nice lad, but he'd been brought up in such a negative atmosphere that he thought this was the way people behaved. He's since modified his behaviour and is more confident himself, and Lucy's confidence gradually came back once she was away from his toxic attitude.

Using confident body language

Stature is really important in conveying confidence. When you're feeling exposed, you have a tendency to cower and cover your vulnerable areas, for example your throat or genitals, which in turn makes you look like you lack confidence (see Figure 5-3).

Figure 5-3: Lacking confidence.

Instead, stand with your head up, shoulders back, stomach tucked in, bottom tucked under, and eyes straight ahead to look super confident – see Figure 5-4.

Eye contact is key to looking confident. Avoiding someone's gaze makes you look shifty or untrustworthy, and you won't be completely aware of what's going on. Maintain eye contact to both look and feel more confident.

Figure 5-4: Oozing confidence.

Sounding confident

After your appearance, your *tonality*, or the sound of your voice, is the second biggest factor in creating your first impression. It's vitally important to how people perceive you. If you look great but talk in a high-pitched nasal whine, people will form a poor impression of you and your confidence will be dented. Most of us are blissfully unaware of the sound or impact of our own voices because we don't actively listen to them.

Talking very quietly when you first meet someone smacks of no or low confidence. Barking at people in a loud voice can be construed as arrogance and a need to be the centre of attention. You need to be able to adjust your volume to suit the occasion.

Watch how people respond to you when you talk. If they're asking you to repeat yourself or they don't respond appropriately to something sad or funny, then you're probably talking too quietly. If they're leaning away from you and the conversation isn't reciprocal, that is, you're dominating it, then they've probably given up as you're too loud. Be sensitive to the nuances of conversation and adjust your volume, proximity, or position to suit the person you're with.

 If you're quietly spoken, practise singing nursery rhymes very loudly and then speak slightly louder than normal. Your internal volume control eventually adjusts to a louder setting. You can also try playing with the volume of your voice to see how different people react. For example, in an argument when you're shouting, quickly change the volume. The impact might be to sound more menacing than angry.

Making people listen

The voice is a very powerful tool; when you talk you want people to listen. A range of atmospheres can be created using your voice alone, and what you say isn't as important as how you say it.

 You don't have to shout to get people's attention in a conversation. Instead, use your proximity and eye contact:

- **Drop your voice slightly** so they have to quieten down and lean in to hear you, then go back to your normal volume when you have their undivided attention.

- **Maintain eye contact when you talk.** The person doing the talking usually makes less eye contact, so you establish a more powerful connection by doing so. Choose your conversation carefully; talking about something contentious may make you appear confrontational. Talking about an intimate subject can be very sexy.

- **Lean in when you talk** to increase the rapport in a conversation and be more captivating.

Making your voice sound attractive

A well-rounded, modulated voice is the most attractive to listen to. We spend a fortune on products to make us look and smell attractive, yet how many people do you know who've invested in making their voice, one of the most powerful assets we possess, sound good?

Sounds right

John was writing a letter to an important client and he asked Elizabeth for some help with the spelling. Elizabeth had never claimed that she'd won prizes for her spelling but, in the absence of a dictionary, she offered her opinion. When John saw the client, they pointed out all his spelling errors. He ranted at Elizabeth. Bemused, she offered the defence that she never claimed to know how to spell the words correctly. 'But you sounded so confident, I assumed your spellings were right,' he fumed.

People have much more confidence in you, your abilities, and your credibility if you 'sound' confident.

The voice is generated by a group of muscles, and like any muscle they need working on to be defined and strong. Here are some ideas:

- ✔ **Record yourself reading out loud.** Analyse the recording. Be careful not to say, 'this is rubbish; I sound horrible; my accent stinks' and focus on thinking 'How can I improve my voice?' Could you improve your *diction* – how clearly you actually say words – or your breathing technique?

  Shallow breathers often sound raspy or rushed in long sentences and also take faster breaths when nervous or anxious, which can make them appear less confident or flustered. By practising taking bigger, deeper, longer-lasting breaths you can gain more control over the length of sentences you can say and have a more stable-sounding voice.

- ✔ **Become involved in a local college or hospital radio station.** The experience will be invaluable, because it will force you to improve the quality of your voice and speech, build your confidence by speaking publicly, you'll meet lots of new people, and possibly have the opportunity for a good flirt!

Avoid smoking! Not only is smoking bad for you health and a passion killer on the breath, it's extremely bad for your voice.

Watch your favourite romantic film and listen to how the actors lower their voices when the mood becomes more intimate or when they're gaining the interest of the opposite sex.

Your diaphragm drives the power in your voice. Good posture is essential for creating a confident, well-projected (not necessarily loud) sound. Any slumping or sagging seriously affects how confident you sound. Adopting a confident stance (refer to Figure 5-4), both when standing and sitting, means you'll sound great.

Improve your diaphragmatic control by lying on your back with a large book placed over your abdomen. When you breathe in, take the breath right down through your lungs and into your stomach so your abdomen inflates and raises the book in the air; then let the air out slowly and make a long continuous note. Try to keep the quality of the note constant all the way through the breath.

Chapter 6

Spotting Who's Available

In This Chapter
▶ Finding single people
▶ Considering tried and tested options
▶ Checking out who's out there

*W*ant to know how to both increase your flirting hit rate *and* boost your confidence with the opposite sex? Avoid the common mistake of chasing after people you fancy before finding out whether they're available to flirt with. The key to flirting success is taking a more strategic approach.

Looking at the traditional flirting grounds as well as exploring some new ones, along with flirting blind, creates an abundance of opportunities for you to enjoy exploring as you develop your flirting prowess.

Knowing Where to Find Other Singletons

Flirting is a game for at least two people. Learning it from a book is all very well but you've got to actually get out there and flirt for real. Excuses like you don't know anyone you want to flirt with or you never meet any new people just don't cut it. The following sections list several of the places where you can find other singletons to flirt with.

Looking for love in the office

If you work in a small office, perhaps by yourself, don't despair – you still have customers, suppliers, and so on to flirt with. If, however, you work in a large or shared building, key places to spot singletons are by the vending machines, office kitchen, canteen, sandwich delivery van, smokers' corner, and entrance to the building.

Hearts on fire

Sam noticed a rather luscious man wandering around the building checking the extinguishers. A quick call to reception confirmed that he was a fireman doing an inspection. The combination of gorgeous and fireman was too much to resist. Sam made excuses to be where he was but didn't have the nerve to try and engage with him. Teased by her friends later for not taking the opportunity when she had it, one of her more rebellious colleagues offered to set off the alarm to see if he'd come back. Unfortunately, the alarm was linked directly to the fire station and a whole crew arrived. Sam's hunky fireman wasn't among them, but another took her eye, and while they waited for the all clear to re-enter the building, she took her opportunity to strike up a conversation, which later led to a date. Her friend meanwhile faced a disciplinary for setting off the alarm.

Avoid missing opportunities by striking while the iron's hot – unless you have a friend who's prepared to risk their career for you!

Even if you don't smoke, lots of flirting and business is done in smokers' corner. Take a break from the grind and have a mingle – you may improve more than your love life.

For more information on how to flirt with colleagues, see Chapter 4.

Flirting in bars

Flirting in bars is generally easier than flirting in a supermarket or in church because people expect to be approached in this socially interactive environment.

Keep these points in mind:

- ✔ Choosing the right bar for you is the first step to finding the right sort of singletons. If football isn't your cup of tea, for example, then avoid sports bars streaming live TV. Look for somewhere that has a mixed clientele, of your age demographic, and that has a reputation for being safe. If you don't know the area, ask people who seem like you for a recommendation.

- ✔ Flirting moves faster in bars than in any other environment (with the exception of the Internet – see the section 'Flirting on the Internet' later in this chapter), so go with the flow and don't be coy. If someone doesn't want to be approached, they'll make it very obvious from the outset by not returning your eye contact, smiles, or conversation. They may even turn or angle away from you just to leave you in no doubt that they're not up for a flirtation with you.

Studying in Newcastle-upon-Tyne gave me a fantastic grounding in flirting in bars – it's practically part of the culture. If you're lucky enough to live somewhere where the crack is all part of the night out experience, flirting in bars is much easier. Newcastle isn't heralded as offering one of Europe's top ten nights out without good reason.

Check out Chapter 19 for tips on how to stay safe when flirting.

After you choose the right venue, use all the tips in Chapter 7 on making an entrance to give yourself the heads up over your flirting rivals.

Enjoying unexpected flirting situations

Any place that people congregate offers flirting potential, so don't limit yourself to flirting in the obvious places such as at work or in bars. Other places where you can be flirtatious include, but aren't restricted to:

- ✔ Supermarkets – checkout staff and other shoppers.

- ✔ Hotels – other customers, and bar and restaurant staff.

- ✔ Planes, trains, and automobiles – other commuters and fellow travellers.

  Contrary to popular belief, you can strike up a flirtation with a commuter, but usually only if you're a stranger on their route. Commuters tend not to entertain dialogue with familiar faces in case they don't like the person and are then forced to either speak to or avoid them for years to come. Occasionally, regular commuters get talking and end up married, but you need to read the signs to tell whether someone wants to be spoken to or not.

- ✔ Parks – any other park visitors, such as dog walkers and people with children.

- ✔ Gyms – fellow gym goers.

- ✔ Anywhere a queue gathers or where you find a congregation – at a protest, the social after church, band or choir practice, sporting events, or the beach.

Barred from flirting

Marc had given up on trying to flirt in bars; one minute nobody seemed available to flirt with, but the next, all the available women were spoken for. Marc's problem was his positioning in the bar. He always sat in a corner, with his back to the action. Not only was he missing the available women, he was also making himself invisible and removing his presence from the flirting radar. By moving nearer the thick of things and facing outward, he instantly joined the flirting throng. He was immediately able to spot people to flirt with *and* he was approached by people eager to flirt with him.

If flirting in bars hasn't worked for you in the past, check out your positioning to see if it's holding you back from joining the flirting fun.

Unlike bars, where people expect to be approached, someone may miss your subtle attempt at flirting in an unexpected situation, so catching their attention may take longer. In these situations, the onus is upon you to act. Use eye contact and some of the other strategies outlined in Chapter 5, and the opportunities will present themselves.

You never know where a friendly flirt will lead or to whom the person you're flirting with could introduce you. You may know of the idea that only six degrees of separation are present between you and everyone else on the planet. If you're one step away from everyone you know and two steps away from everyone they know, then the whole planet is only six steps away from each other. Therefore, it follows that you're only a matter of a few steps away from your perfect flirtation.

Flirting on the Internet

The Internet is teeming with opportunities to meet people from all over the world. Internet flirting is more adventurous and fast paced than face-to-face flirting for three reasons:

✔ You don't risk face-to-face rejection.

✔ Physical chemistry is irrelevant.

✔ Using the written word rather than body language allows you to be more direct and explicit and to make your intentions clear.

A walk on the wild side

Jo and her friends went to Blackpool for a girly weekend. Not knowing the area, they asked the taxi driver to drop them at a bar. They wandered in, decked up to the nines, to be greeted by a bar full of elderly gents with barely a set of teeth between them – and all mad keen to buy them a drink. Escaping across the road to another club, they realised the men were more beautifully made up than they were. A friendly chat with the doorman eventually led them away from the transvestite club and to the kind of venue frequented by the sort of men they did want to meet, and everyone had a great night.

If you don't want to be disappointed, do your homework first to find the right bar.

Where to look

Use an established site, such as www.match.com or www.friends reuniteddating.co.uk, to try Internet flirting. If you use a social networking site, such as Facebook or MySpace, you can ask a friend to give you an online introduction to someone you like the look of on their page.

Forums and chatrooms offer lots of opportunities for online flirting – anyone can find the niche they're looking for. If you work in human resources, for example, you can log on and join forums such as www.CIPD.co.uk, www.Trainingzone.co.uk, and www.HrZone.co.uk. Professionals can contact other professionals on the www.LinkedIn.com forum. Not only are you building your virtual network, you're also building a rapport with people with similar interests. You can find forums and chatrooms on www.MSN.com, www.Yahoo.com, and so on and can search by location or interest when looking for people to meet.

Unlike dating sites, you can't guarantee that the people you meet in chatrooms or on forums are single or looking, but you can be sure to meet lots of people you have something in common with.

How to communicate

Getting the language right is an art when it comes to online flirting. Keep these points in mind:

> ✔ Poor grammar and spelling can be a big turn off because recipients may think you're not too bright. If you type quickly, always proof read your message before posting it.

✔ Coming on too strong may be interpreted as wanting to sleep with the person on the first date. Keep your online flirting light and fun. If you're going to eventually entice the person on a first date, you need to maintain their interest.

Humour is your greatest ally for online flirting. Some people find being funny much easier in print because timing isn't an issue, and nor is stony silence or polite laughter if the other person doesn't find your message funny.

✔ Don't worry about writing long messages; most people can decide in a few sentences whether they like your style. Offering the odd compliment on their picture or writing style is just as effective online as in the flesh.

✔ Always post a recent picture and only use a sexy screen name if you're prepared for people looking for sexy connections to pursue you.

Familiarise yourself with the safety tips in Chapter 19 before you launch your Internet flirting campaign.

Telling Who's Available and Who's Interested

Checking out someone's availability needs to be your first priority before launching into anything more than a friendly flirt to avoid wasting your time and effort. Flirting with available people yields a much higher success rate. (Of course, this isn't such a problem if you've found someone on a singles' site; by virtue of being on it you should be pretty secure in knowing that they're available.)

Once you know that someone's available, you next need to decide how much effort to put into pursuing them. To make that decision, you need to be able to tell how interested the other person is.

Assessing and tackling the stances people take

People generally take one of four stances when being flirted with, as the following sections explain. In addition to describing the characteristics associated with these stances, I also provide strategies you can use for each type. Following the advice here will improve your flirting hit rate enormously.

The wallflower

The wallflower loiters at the sides of a room or the back of a group, watching the action and waiting for you to make the move to include them in the fun. You can certainly find easier types to flirt with than the wallflower, but here's what to do if other types aren't available. Be prepared to do all the running, and don't give up on first eye contact. If they're not making much eye contact generally, encourage them to make more with your own use of facial language: lots of smiling, changes in expression, head nods, tilts, and so on. Flirting with a wallflower is slow work – they need your words and gestures to offer lots of encouragement and reassurance that you like them.

The fence sitter

The fence sitter hangs on the periphery at social events, interjecting when he or she feels comfortable doing so. Fence sitters won't declare their hand unless they're sure you fancy them.

Fence sitters are fairly easy to flirt with, but beware of the following to make the flirt a successful one. If a fence sitter is into you, you'll be able to tell quite quickly, but only once you've declared your hand. After you've made it obvious that you like them, though, the good news is that they'll jump right in. Expressive facial language and subtle compliments are necessary to encourage the fence sitter to get the hint.

The egoist

The egoist likes to be the centre of attention and for you to be hanging on their every word and reciprocating all their body language advances. Egoists are the easiest to flirt with and the quickest to strike up a rapport.

Flirting with an egoist is easy. Give them lots of eye contact, let them do the talking as they enjoy the sound of their own voice, laugh at their jokes, and smile a lot. The downside of egoists is that working out if you're just another flirtation or somebody special to them is difficult because they're flirtatious with everybody. If an egoist really likes you, they'll eventually let you do the talking.

The already-spoken-for

Usually in a relationship already, this person may be happy to flirt without intent or may not flirt at all. For people already in relationships to flirt with others isn't uncommon, and the already-spoken-for is easy to flirt with if you're looking for a full-on flirtation. Flirting may provide them with recognition, affection, excitement, and so on. Making polite, interested conversation and not letting them feel you're hitting on them is the best approach.

If you're confused as to why I've included this type, I've spent years watching people trying to flirt furiously with them to no avail, but the plus side is that you can often use already-spoken-fors as a great route to an introduction to their mate, who is available.

Spotting availability from afar

Telling if someone is available isn't as difficult as it sounds. You can use clues such as their dress and posture to determine who will and won't be receptive to your flirtation. Ideally, you'll make the initial determination from afar.

Dressing to impress

Being well dressed or better dressed than usual (if you already know the person) is a good indicator of intent. If you've never met them before, are they better dressed than others in the immediate social environment? If so, they've made a special effort in order to feel good about themselves and impress the other people gathered.

Posturing

A person's posture can give clues to how receptive they are to being approached. If the object of your desire is a woman, look for a curvy posture. Women either cross their legs with the toe of their shoe pointing at the person they fancy, or dangle their shoe from their toe, as in Figure 6-1. If they stand up, they place more of their weight on one leg than the other to create a curvy effect. In men, watch for drawing themselves up to their full height, with their legs apart, widening their stance, leading from the crotch, and possibly pointing their thumbs towards their crotch, as in Figure 6-1. Both men and women put their shoulders back to expose their chests. They may also raise their heads to expose the soft underside of the throat – exposing vulnerable areas of the body is provocative.

Preening

Playing with hair – stroking it down for men or tossing and playing with it for women – is a key sign of availability. Adjusting your clothes while looking at the other person, wetting, licking, or biting your lips, or putting objects or fingers in the mouth or self touching are also highly sexual (see Figure 6-2). Preening is unusual body language and thus attracts attention.

Figure 6-1: Male and female signals of availability.

Figure 6-2: Girl mouth gesture.

Eye scouting

Available people scan the room to see who's available and to check out who's looking at them. This move is a fairly slow scan of the room. If you see someone scanning round in a quick flash they're more likely to be looking for someone they know.

Knowing if they're interested

After you've established someone's availability, test to see if they're interested. Initially, do this from a distance in order to test the waters without risking a face-to-face rejection.

If you've been playing with eye contact and flashes (explained in Chapter 7), now's the time to ramp it up. Catch their eye, hold it for up to four seconds, long enough for them to know you're definitely looking at *them*, then momentarily look away and back again. Follow up this little routine with an eyebrow flash and a smile. If they reciprocate, you're at first base.

If the person you're flirting with has a little preen, either adjusting their clothes or toying with their hair or necklace (as in Figure 6-3) for example (you can find other preening signs in the preceding section), they're letting you know they're interested. You can now safely begin a face-to-face approach. Go to Chapter 7 for information on making the first move.

Figure 6-3: Guy grooming.

It ain't easy being cheesy

I was working on a show with a TV presenter and some of the contestants were getting to grips with flirting body language. They were a youngish group of contestants and refused to believe that eye contact was the most effective way to make contact with someone you want to flirt with. This particular presenter was recently single and confessed to them that she'd used all my tips and, although she felt really cheesy using the four-second eye contact routine, it worked every time.

Letting an Ad or Agency Help You Connect

The dating industry is a multi-million pound industry and growing. With society being so time poor and expectations of a potential mate so high, the dating industry is capitalising on the fact that most people don't have the time or desire to evaluate every person they meet to see if they're suitable. Ideally, agencies take the legwork out of the process and present you with a selection of potentially perfect candidates for your affections.

Check out the tips in Chapter 19 to ensure you play safe.

Scouring lonely hearts ads

Most papers offer a 'would like to meet' section, which is perfect for people who don't want to invest a lot of money in finding other singletons.

Check the publication's readership to get an idea of the types of people who are likely to place and respond to ads. Choosing one that matches your interests and values is more likely to lead you to singletons with whom you have something in common.

Responding to an advert

Recording your message for your advert is generally free – you just call a free phone number. However, you pay a premium rate to leave messages in response to an advert and to collect the messages left for your ad.

Be aware that ads can remain live for longer than the person is looking. So don't worry if the ad-poster doesn't reply; you don't know when the ad was posted and if they're still checking messages.

Lost in lecturing

Steven worked in a university, but despite trying everything from speed-dating to blind dates, he couldn't find anyone he found attractive. He spoke to the person running the speed-dating session to complain and they offered him a free session. Before the session the organisers checked out the female attendees and were quite happy that they were all attractive and in different ways. To their surprise, none of them even remotely registered as interesting to Steven. Finally, it transpired that Steven refused to flirt with someone unless he thought they were going to be 'the one'. The organiser explained that you have to kiss a few frogs before you find 'the one' and friendly flirting was a great way to get to know a frog before you get to the tonsil hockey stage. Steven decided to give it a go and before he knew it he was surrounded by flirting opportunities. Working in a university gave him plenty of colleagues and staff to choose from. Before he knew it he was well into his flirting zone and eventually found a frog that met his specifications.

Open your eyes to the opportunities that surround you to get your flirting momentum going.

Aim to sound attractive when recording or leaving a message. Practise your message in a sing-song manner to improve the dynamic sound of your voice. You may feel ridiculous, but as these recordings are generally such poor quality, using this tone actually sounds more 'normal'.

Setting up an advert yourself

Some publications allow you to set up ads attracting written responses – but charge a fee for the privilege. You only get what you pay for when it comes to lonely hearts ads.

Don't reinvent the wheel when writing your own ad. Have a look at the ads you find most eye catching, then craft yours along the same lines.

Speed-dating for instant results

Speed-dating first appeared at the turn of this century, which makes it a relatively recent addition to the dating options available. In a speed-dating scenario, you have a string of mini dates in the space of a few hours. You mark on a chart whether you'd like to see the person again or not, and after the event the organiser contacts you with mutual responses. Speed-dating is an inexpensive way of meeting lots of dates in a very short period of time. For your nearest speed-dating event, try searching on the Internet for speed-dating in your area.

Second time lucky?

Being unsure of what type of agency to try, John joined an events agency. As he walked through the door, the women outnumbered the men and they all looked keen to get to know him. He endured an exhausting evening of the competitive women and was glad when it was time to escape. John didn't have the time or the stomach to trawl events, but he did have the cash to pay someone to find him a suitable singleton. He did his research this time and asked the agencies about the types of women on their books and the matching process they used. Soon, John was presented with hand-picked singletons to date at a more relaxed pace.

Don't plump for the first agency you stumble across. Check out all the options to find the right solution for you – and your wallet.

Niche speed-dating events cover everything from religion, sexual orientation, age, geographical location, career, and even hobbies. A group of speed-daters definitely exists out there for you.

Speed-dating's main appeal is the ability it offers to jump straight in. Other benefits include:

- ✔ You can check for chemistry.

- ✔ You can look for things in common.

- ✔ Events are inexpensive.

- ✔ Face-to-face rejection is unlikely.

- ✔ You don't need to make a commitment.

- ✔ You only have to spend a few minutes with a person if you're not attracted to them.

- ✔ Your response rate (in other words, the number of mutual matches you make at the event) signals to you how attractive you are to other singletons.

Speed-dating resembles going on job interviews: the more you do, the better you get.

Getting the best results from speed-dating requires a bit of preparation. Check the dress code with the organiser first to make sure you look the part, and prepare some conversation openers (see Chapter 8). Smile a lot, use plenty of eye contact, and be yourself – your speed-dating will be a piece of cake.

Looking at dating agencies

If you've tried introduction or dating agencies in the past and had no joy, try again now. The dating agency landscape is constantly changing; key players and reputations shift as technology evolves and people seek more niche agencies.

Choosing the right service for you saves you time and money in the long term. The more the agency does, the more expensive it is. In the following list, the more expensive services are at the top and the cheaper options are at the bottom. The types of approach are broken down into the following areas:

- ✔ **Headhunting services:** A personal search agent finds you a partner.

- ✔ **Personal introductions:** A member of staff introduces you to likely partners.

- ✔ **Events:** An agency sets up social occasions for singletons.

- ✔ **Computer comparisons:** Your details are entered onto a database and a computer program matches you to someone with similar characteristics and interests.

- ✔ **Lists:** You're given a list of all, or selected, clients when you join the agency and at regular intervals during membership.

Visit the Association of British Introduction Agencies (www.abia.org.uk) for more information.

Chapter 7

Making an Entrance

In This Chapter

▶ Turning heads

▶ Grabbing the limelight

▶ Taking the initiative

*M*aking an entrance is one of the most under-rated, but effective, tricks in the book. Rather than you having to do all the running, it gives everyone who's on the lookout a good chance to view you at your best and increases the chance of attracting even more people to flirt with you. This chapter gives you the details.

Ta-da!

Stars make head-turning entrances for a reason – to catch the attention of everyone around them. Making a fabulous entrance grabs the attention of the person you want to impress and makes others sit up and pay attention. You can use an entrance not only to produce great flirting but also professional results, too. A confident entrance impresses clients as well as colleagues, so use it at every opportunity. Standing out from the crowd from the point you enter a room is your key objective.

I teach the following entrance not only for people on the pull but for business networking, too. Making a great entrance is one of the easiest ways of drawing people to you. Learn and execute the following whenever you make an entrance:

- ✔ Start every entrance with a pause. Bursting or stumbling into a room isn't classy.

- ✔ Use the pause to gather yourself to your full height, then pull your shoulders back, stick your chest out, hold your stomach in, lift your head up, and look straight ahead.

✔ Look to the busiest part of the room and smile, even if you don't know anybody. People see you smiling and think you are a popular, approachable person, and you stay on their radar all evening as someone worth talking to.

✔ Make your way slowly, but statuesquely, towards the busiest part of the room, giving the people looking the best chance to take you in.

✔ Make eye contact as you scan the room. You'll see the people who are watching – they're the ones who are curious or available.

Turning heads with body language

Would the paparazzi be chasing Brad Pitt or Angelina Jolie up the red carpet if they moved like Homer and Marge Simpson? Not likely. Body language that's different to the norm grabs attention. Strong, definite movements, for example, demonstrate confidence, which in turn serves as both a magnet for other people and as an aphrodisiac. (You can read more on confidence in Chapter 5). People who exhibit definite body language and distinctive movements, as well as those who move differently as a result of disability, for example, stand out.

Flick through a magazine and you'll see celebrities all exhibiting the same body language. You'll never see these people slouching or with their heads down – unless they're in disgrace or caught off guard by the paparazzi. Use star body language by doing the following:

✔ **Always hold your head up, with an elongated neck, and keep your eyes looking straight ahead:** This pose demonstrates an aura of control, authority, and sexuality.

✔ **Keep your shoulders back and your chest out:** By exposing your chest (a vulnerable part of your body), you're inviting people to come to you. You're pulling people into you as if your chest were a fisherman's line.

Control underwear can improve posture in both men and women. This miracle gear pulls the wearer up and in, creating a firm, fit, and sexually appealing figure, eliminating muffin tops, creating a perter bottom, and even creating a sleeker torso for men when wearing a whole undershirt. A good website for finding out more about control underwear is www. themagicknickershop.co.uk.

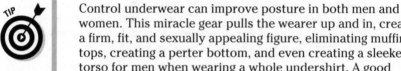

✔ **Scan the room slowly and don't dart your gaze away from eye contact:** A slow, steady scan of the room indicates that you're confident and controlled enough to stand still and take in your surroundings before choosing which person or group you'll go to.

Figures 7-1 and 7-2 demonstrate the differences between ordinary and star body language.

Figure 7-1: Ordinary body language.

Figure 7-2: Star body language.

Let me in!

Carl was at a conference. He was taken with another delegate but wasn't having much luck catching her eye. On the first day he spotted the restaurant but was struggling to open the door until somebody opened it from the other side and he fell headlong into the room, drawing quiet sniggers from the other diners. Rather than head through the middle of the room he decided not to draw attention to himself and crept his way around the walls, until his backside knocked a trolley and its entire contents off balance, sending it crashing to the floor. By now the other diners were in fits of laughter and gave him a round of applause, much to his mortification.

Determined not to repeat this experience, Carl attended a course on body language and by the next conference had perfected his entrance. He paused and composed himself before making a head-turning entrance at every opportunity. 'Haven't we met somewhere before?' asked a woman with a flirtatious smile. She had, but Carl wasn't going to remind her that it was his disastrous restaurant entrance a few months back. He turned more heads that conference and was never short of company, *and* he caught the interest of the woman he'd fancied at the previous event.

Never miss an opportunity to make a great entrance to draw flirting opportunities to you like a magnet.

Navigating stairs

Don't think of stairs as simply being a vehicle to get from one area to another; they're a prime opportunity for you to out dazzle everyone else in the room.

1. **Hold your position before taking the first step to steady yourself.** This pause is especially important for women in high heels.

2. **Judge how much distance there is between the steps to ensure a smooth descent.**

3. **Lead with your toe.**

4. **Keep your head up (no looking down when you're into your descent!).** You need your peripheral vision to be alert, to judge what's going on beneath your feet and possible hazards such as carpets, slippery floors, uneven steps, and so on.

Sandra's secret helper

Sandra wasn't feeling too confident about the Christmas party she had to attend so she splashed out on a pair of Spanx (`www.spanx.com`) that went from her bust down to her knees. These giant pants weren't the sexiest of undergarments, but they made her feel fantastic and gave her a better shape. She flounced her way down the stairs to the hotel lounge, eyes straight ahead and exuding bags of confidence. Over the course of the evening she was approached by several people who all used the same opening line, 'I couldn't help but notice you when you walked down the stairs . . .' Clearly, she was not going to be short of company and could take her pick of the men.

Remember, even Marilyn Monroe wore a girdle. Get yourself some confidence-boosting underwear and combine it with a well-practised stair descent to get heads turning and the compliments flowing.

 Watch an old movie and see how starlets like Marilyn Monroe and the James Bond characters perfected descending a staircase with effortless grace and head-turning style – then practise on your own stairs. Get a friend to video you walking down the stairs; spot your mistakes and work on them until you can descend like they do in the movies.

Positioning Yourself for Maximum Effect

Your star body language (see 'Turning heads with body language' earlier in this chapter) grabs attention, but positioning yourself in the right spots doubles the effect and turns you into a magnet for people who are on the look out for a flirtation.

Big-time stars don't skulk along the perimeter or hide behind pillars, they deliberately position themselves in the prime spots to show their best sides and create great viewing opportunities for everyone. Actors always fight for centre stage with good reason: this spot gives them the most limelight and keeps them the focus of the audience's attention. If you want to engage with the maximum number of people to the best effect, you have to position yourself in the right space in the room.

Choosing power spots

A power spot is one where you can see what's going on and as many people as possible can get a good view of you.

Where you can see the doors and other busy places

In business, the best seat in the room is the one farthest from the door and with the best view of it; the most vulnerable position is right behind the door with your back to it. Studies show that people sitting with their back to the door in business meetings, offices, or restaurants have a higher respiratory rate and are therefore more anxious than people facing the door.

In bars and clubs, single people have one eye on the entrance and the other on the toilet, as these areas see the most movement and they can check out the people on the move without being watched themselves. Prominent stairs between floors are also hot areas to watch.

Watching the door is a primitive safety response. Cavemen sat with their backs to the wall of the cave, facing the fire and entrance and watching for danger. These days we don't have to fear being ambushed by a sabre-toothed tiger, but we are alert to the comings and goings in a room.

Other power spots

You can find power spots in almost any situation. Here I list a few examples:

- ✔ **Sitting next to the host or hostess at a dinner party.** This demonstrates that you're in a favoured position.

- ✔ **Standing next to the guest of honour.** As the other invitees want to gain the attention of the honoured guest, being next to that person puts you in the line of vision to be seen and admired as well. You're reflected in the other person's power.

- ✔ **Sitting at the head of the table.** Having the top position makes it clear that you have a higher status than anyone else at the table, making you a more attractive flirting prospect.

- ✔ **Positioning yourself with your back to a window.** By having the sun at your back you cast yourself in the shadows. You're then able to see the facial expressions of the person in front of you, although they can't see yours. This position is a powerful one when you want to observe someone before revealing too much of yourself.

Positions to avoid

Your position can place you anywhere from being invisible to being the focus of the room. Avoid the following positions at all costs:

- ✔ **Around the walls of the room.** Here you blend in with the wallpaper and become invisible behind the crowds in front of you.

- ✔ **Behind the door.** Here you can't see who's coming or going and nobody will spot you because you're obscured every time the door opens.

- ✔ **With your back to the busiest part of the room.** The busiest part of the room is where all the action is. If you can't see it and the people there can't see you, you're missing the bulk of the flirting opportunities.

- ✔ **Corners of rooms.** Nobody likes to be cornered and people aren't at their most comfortable approaching someone in a corner, so avoid loitering there.

Knowing when to move

The best power spot in a room at 8 p.m. may not be the same at 11 p.m. Factors affecting the best place to stand are:

- ✔ **Changing light:** The dimmer the lighting, the more seductive the atmosphere. Candlelight, for example, is very flattering to the complexion and conducive to romance.

- ✔ **Changing numbers of people in the room:** You don't want to be left in a quiet spot, so keep moving to where the action is.

- ✔ **Congregation spots:** When people first enter a room they may congregate at the cloakroom, then move to the bar, to the centre of the room, and then you may see a steady flow around the room or to the toilet, and so on. Be prepared to go with the flow to keep yourself in the limelight.

- ✔ **Noise levels:** An optimum level of background noise is conducive to connecting with people and making conversation. If the background noise is too loud in a room, chatting without breaching someone else's personal space too soon is difficult. If it's too quiet, people are put off making conversation.

If you're out with a group of people and you can let them know in advance that you're in the mood to go flirting, a subtle nod that it's time to move usually does the job for staying in the hottest spot in the room. If you're looking to flirt discreetly and you can't tell your friends that you're doing so, make an excuse to pop to the loo and take the busiest route there. You should be able to use your flirting radar to spot the signs of other single people looking to meet others, so you could buddy up with another singleton to keep you company while you're moving around on the look out.

Making the First Move

So you've perfected your star moves and found the power spots in the room. You could then just wait for someone to spot you. For a higher flirting success rate, though, you can take the initiative and make the first move. Not only will the other person be flattered that you've approached them, you'll be calling the shots and be in control of the situation, instead of hanging around hoping that the other person makes their move before the opportunity has gone!

Using your eyebrows

The eyebrows are marvellous for letting somebody know that you've spotted them from a distance, usually from a stationary position in the social zone (1.2–1.8 metres) or beyond, or when passing each other. An eyebrow flash – a quick raising of both eyebrows – is a non-sexual advance that works on both sexes. Eyebrow flashes are a universal greeting, a non-verbal hello, and are completely safe to use, except in Japan where they have sexual connotations.

The marvellous thing about an eyebrow flash is that it usually gets reciprocated (if the other person spots it) and registers you on a subconscious level with that person as someone who is friendly and approachable. An eyebrow flash is the perfect preamble to a smile and isn't as risky as beaming from a standing start at someone, wondering if they're going to reciprocate.

 If your eyebrow flash isn't reciprocated, you could be too far away for the other person to see it. Try moving closer, and if they still don't reciprocate then they're probably not that interested or just very short sighted.

 Raising just one eyebrow at a time can indicate anything from a leer to questioning or mistrust, so stick with the double eyebrow raise to create that vital positive first impression.

Knowing when to speak

To maximise your chances of a successful flirt you have to accomplish several milestones before you actually speak a word to the other person:

1. **The eyebrow flash:** You need the other person to reciprocate.

2. **The four-second glance:** Look at the person for four seconds, look away, and then look back. If they're still looking, they're interested. (Omit this step if you're flirting for new friends as opposed to finding dates.)

3. **The smile:** Nobody can resist a smile and if the other person has reciprocated the other step(s), a good chance exists that the smile will be successfully reciprocated, too.

Only after you've completed this non-verbal hello can you approach to speak and be virtually guaranteed a positive response from the other person. Speaking without ensuring you've put in this groundwork first leaves you open to the risk of rejection at close quarters, whereas if the other person doesn't return your eyebrow flashes or smiles no harm is done, you've not put yourself on the line, and you have no public rejection to endure.

Using icebreakers

People worry disproportionately about what they're going to say to break the ice at the start of a flirtation and try and come up with clever or convoluted opening lines to make themselves appear more interesting. Indeed, making the opening gambit is often the most nerve-wracking part of a flirtation and the area where you can feel most at risk of rejection or of making a fool of yourself. However, you can minimise this risk.

Icebreaker is a very apt description for the line you use to break into a conversation with someone, but having successfully applied your non-verbal hello, delivering an icebreaker is more akin to scraping the frost off a windscreen than having to hammer through a sturdy surface. By training yourself to focus on the step before the icebreaker, you can reposition your nerves and angst towards icebreakers and view them as the next step in a logical process, as opposed to a terrifying leap.

You can choose from three different types of icebreakers, picking the one that best suits your personality type:

✔ **Scenario icebreakers, for the creative flirt:** You can use these when you're creating a situation as the excuse to make the icebreaker. For example, 'I'm looking for my friend. I was supposed to be meeting her here; have you seen a short, blonde girl in a pink dress?' This approach works because it's non-threatening and gives the other person an excuse to speak to you while you wait for your friend (whether the friend exists or not, or has just popped to the loo).

✔ **Compliment icebreakers, for the confident flirt:** If you've had a really good response to your non-verbal hello, you could just launch in with a compliment, such as 'You've got a great smile. I just thought I'd come and introduce myself.' This approach works because the other person has given you an enthusiastic response to your non-verbal hello, and with your compliment you've confirmed that you find them attractive.

✔ **Introduction icebreakers, for the conventional flirt:** This approach is very straightforward, non-threatening, and a bit formal. You simply approach the other person, offer them a handshake, and say 'Hi, I'm Susan. Pleased to meet you'. Convention dictates that they'll then reciprocate.

If networking is part of your job, practise the steps in the earlier 'Knowing when to speak' section and follow them in practice with a simple introductory 'Hi! I'm Charlie. May I join you?' icebreaker. You'll be amazed how easy breaking the ice with strangers becomes. When you're out shopping and meeting strangers, try following that opener with 'Could you recommend somewhere that does a great coffee?'

An icebreaker is simply a pretext to talking to someone. To deliver it confidently and follow the conversation codes in Chapter 8, ensuring that you get the conversation started easily and running smoothly, keep it simple. You can also benefit from practising on friendly flirts to improve your delivery and confidence when it comes to romantic flirtations. I've included more opening lines in Chapter 16 to give you some ideas.

Chapter 8

Making Conversation with Absolutely Anybody

In This Chapter

▶ Mastering the art of conversation

▶ Making the opening move

▶ Telling if they're enjoying the chat

Starting a conversation, particularly with a stranger, is something that many people find daunting – and particularly so when they're attracted to them. Don't worry. You can make not knowing what to say, fluffing your words, or not being able to tell if your listener is wilting with boredom a thing of the past. This chapter gives you all the tools you need to make conversation with everyone, from the neighbour you've never spoken with to strangers you meet in the street and from work colleagues to the object of your desires. Making great conversation shouldn't be saved just for flirting. Make it a way of life and you'll never be short of friends or company.

Understanding Conversational Conventions

A conversation is simply an opportunity to get to know somebody a little better and for them to know you a little better. Social psychologists and anthropologists alike have studied how we make conversation, and while you may be keen to make a show-stopping impression with a dazzling display of wit and general knowledge, research shows that by simply sticking to the conventions of conversation when first initialising contact, your relationships actually get off on a much better footing.

It's a dog's life

Lucy had lived in her street for years and hadn't spoken a word to any of her neigh-bours. When asked to look after her friend's dog, she discovered a whole new instant social circle on her doorstep that she never knew existed. Dog walking etiquette dictates that you say 'Hello' to all other walkers attached to a dog, then, when you've met them several times, you start exchanging doggie information, and finally, make general conversation. She noted that older walkers without dogs also participated in this morning ritual. After two weeks of dog walking, Lucy came to look forward to her cheery morning greetings with her fellow dog walkers; she discovered that the more enthusiastic her 'Hello' or 'Good morning', the more cheery the response it elicited. By the time she returned home from her walk she felt bright and perky and had a smile on her face.

These contacts gave Lucy the confidence to strike up more spontaneous conversa-tions with people she wouldn't normally talk to, like her neighbours and some of her colleagues. Lucy has her own rescue dog now and a rather dashing boyfriend that she met and slowly got to know on her dog walks.

Opportunities to strike up conversations exist everywhere. Take them where you find them to build your confidence and your social circle.

Using opening lines

'I'm here, now what are your other two wishes?' one enthusiastic stranger blurted in my ear when I was least expecting it. Not the best opening line I've ever heard, but surprisingly not the worst either. The point of an opening line is that the other person recognises it as an attempt to initiate conversation. Your conversational opener doesn't have to be contrived, and avoiding chat-up lines is probably best unless you've got lots of experience in delivering them successfully. Sticking to something simple is always the best tactic for initiating any type of conversation.

Avoid using negative language when initiating conversation. A posi-tive attitude is attractive – use it to your advantage.

Offering a simple opener

After you initiate your non-verbal hello, such as eye contact, an eyebrow flash, or smile, choose a very simple opener. 'Hi, do you mind if I join you?' works in situations from networking to pulling. This line may sound a little old fashioned and uninspired, but it requires a response from the other person because you're asking a question. Most people are too polite to say no, and if they've eyebrow flashed you already, they won't anyway. By verbalising a 'yes', they're accepting you on a subconscious level, too. (Find out more about non-verbal hellos and eyebrow flashes in Chapter 7.)

Talking about the weather

Conversations about the weather are very common, particularly in English-speaking countries. Even in places where the weather is fabulous, people have adapted weather talk to suit their climate. Talking about the weather may seem very predictable, but the best openers are the ones where people know how to respond and that can be interpreted as an attempt to open conversation. No pressure is placed on the other person to think of a clever response, hence conversation is easier to make.

When the weather's good, openers are easy. 'Great day, isn't it?', and 'Aren't we having fabulous weather?' are perfect, non-threatening, positive openers, which people instinctively know how to respond to. When the weather's bad, put a positive spin on your opener to avoid appearing negative. Replace 'Isn't the rain awful?' with 'Great weather for ducks!'

Whatever line you choose, what matters is that you've started the conversation. In responding to weather openers, make sure you stick with convention and agree with whatever opener they've just used. Saying 'I prefer it cooler' in response to 'Great weather' instantly strikes a note of discord with the other person. 'Yes, it's great, but a break from the heat wouldn't go amiss' is a better response, as you're agreeing with them and also adding a little extra information about your preferences.

Following up weather openers is simple because lots of conversational threads can follow on, particularly in relation to holidays: 'It was lovely and hot/cold on my holiday in New York; we did, x, y, and z.' These conversations give you the opportunity for personal disclosure, and people are usually happy to discuss holidays and holiday plans.

Use a simple weather opener every day with someone new to build your confidence in initiating conversation.

Making humour work

Entertaining someone with conversation is often misinterpreted as a requirement to tell jokes. We've all been in situations involving grinning and bearing it as someone makes relentless jokes with barely a pause for responses. Joke telling actually prevents a conversation developing and if you waste your precious three to five minutes when someone is forming their opinion of you, you lose an opportunity to discover things you have in common. Not everyone's a natural comedian and even professionals spend hours practising. Lines that sound natural, spontaneous, and hilarious when delivered by a professional comic, are actually thoroughly crafted. Unless you can put this level of dedication into your joke telling, avoid telling jokes when you first meet someone.

The other person doesn't have to be laughing out loud to be entertained. Just aim to initiate interesting conversation on themes that the other person can contribute to (see Chapter 9 for more ideas).

Telling stories about your own experiences that have funny or entertaining endings and which relate to the topics of conversation you're having, instantly builds rapport. The odd joke is fine once you're well into the swing of a conversation, but keep them relevant to the subject and avoid vulgarity and profanities.

Avoiding mentioning the ex!

You're probably no longer with your ex for good reason, otherwise you'd still be together Anyone who wants to empathise with you over the break up will probably bore you just as much with their story as you will them with yours. A time and place exist for ex stories and within an initial conversation/flirtation isn't it!

Avoid people who bring up their ex in an initial flirtation; they're either not over them or thrive on negative vibes. Consider the warning a lucky break and move on to another flirting prospect.

If someone does try to inflict their ex story on you, be careful not to fall into the trap of being their shoulder to cry on. Once you're fulfilling the role of best friend, it becomes very difficult for that person to see you as anything other than a friend. See Chapter 4 for reasons why you want to avoid this scenario.

Diverting the conversation from contentious topics

Talking about sex, religion, or politics is usually a no, no unless you're a vicar or a politician. Remember that the aim of any initial conversation is simply to open it and use it as an opportunity to find out things you have in common. Divisive threads of conversation may give you an opportunity to show off your debating prowess, but whether the other person still wants to speak to you when you've beaten them into submission with your interpretation of the socioeconomic reasons behind the recession, is another matter.

Date or inquisition?

Mark joined a dating agency and was struggling to get past the first date with the women on the books. The agency staff tried to help him perfect his technique. He seemed to be doing everything right and his topics of conversation were well researched and interesting, but they realised that his delivery was ruining his chances. He'd memorised things to talk about so that he didn't run dry, but introduced topics in a series of closed questions. His dates felt like they were being interrogated.

Mark changed his approach. He stuck with the same topics of conversation but used open questions to introduce them. Instead of the conversation running dry and his dates becoming defensive, these questions opened up other avenues of conversation. He became more confident at conversing with women and second dates soon followed. Mark also began using open questions at work and found building rapport with his colleagues much easier.

Use open questions whenever possible to build great rapport.

Divert the conversation away from contentious topics by simply saying, 'That's really interesting, but I never talk about sex/ religion/politics before midnight.' Follow up this line with something light-hearted, possibly related to a topic you've seen on the news, for example 'Talking of current affairs, what do you think of Tony Blair's nose job?'

Building Rapport

Building rapport through personal disclosure and questioning the other person on their preferences is vital in cementing the flirting process.

Honing the art of open questions

Finding out about the other person is the name of the game when building rapport and gives a boost to both your personal and professional relationships. A succession of questions leading to yes or no answers (called *closed questions*) leaves you no opportunity for personal disclosure, which is vital for the other person to find out what things you share. People like people that they have things in common with.

Asking open questions gets you on the fast track to building rapport. So instead of asking a closed question like 'Isn't it cold today?' ask an open question that requires a longer response: 'What do you think of the weather today?'

Open questions start with who, when, what, where, why, or how.

Ask a friend or colleague to count how many open and closed questions you ask in a normal conversation. Aim to improve your rate of posing open questions in your conversations.

Picking a topic that they want to chat on

Building rapport is easier if you're giving the other person the chance to talk on a subject they're interested in. Rather than domineering the conversation with your own interests, listen carefully and probe for their interests. Having a number of options up your sleeve, based on the following tips, is the trick.

Tailor your conversation to the needs of the other person. Just because you enjoy the latest developments of your favourite soap, or the success of your football team's new line up, doesn't necessarily mean that the person you're conversing with finds it equally gripping.

Research shows that women speak more words in a day than men, which accounts for why they find making small talk easier. Men, apparently, are more interested in facts and women in emotions. Below are common topics that you can research and use for both sexes to keep conversations flowing:

- ✔ News headlines (from current affairs to reality TV)
- ✔ Topics, interests, and events from their social media page (such as Facebook, linkedin, MySpace, and so on)
- ✔ Their line of work
- ✔ Planned or previous holiday destinations
- ✔ Musical tastes
- ✔ Interests and hobbies

Preventing conversations from running dry

Stopping conversations from running dry takes practice, but when you know how, you'll never be short of conversation again. As well as being vital for taking the initiative in the flirting arena, keeping conversation going is a fantastic means of gaining the edge over other candidates in a job interview by allowing you to tell the interviewer everything they should know about you.

Look for opportunities to tell people things about yourself based on the information they've just shared with you; it fast tracks your rapport and helps the other person see how much you have in common. People who are good at personal disclosure leave you with the feeling that 'you've known them for years'.

Give expanded responses

Consider the following dialogue: 'Isn't the hot weather great?' ' Yes, I love it when it's hot. I went to Denver on business recently and the climate there is great – hot in summer, cold in winter – and the scenery is fantastic.' This expanded response to the initial question not only tells the other person that you like the heat, but also that you have a job involving foreign travel. You leave the door open for them to ask about your job and where you travel with it. You in turn can then ask about their job and any travel they do. You've instantly both disclosed something about yourselves and the commonalities bring you closer together.

Answering questions with plenty of meaningful information (without hogging the conversation) and with a question tagged onto the end of your response keeps the rapport building and the conversation ping ponging back and forth nicely.

Take inspiration from your surroundings

Use your surroundings to initiate and maintain conversation. If music is playing, comment on it: 'I love this track. I saw this band in concert a couple of years ago and they were brilliant. What concerts have you been to recently?' If you're having a drink, comment on that: 'This coffee smells great. You can't beat a cup of fresh coffee. My day doesn't start until I've had at least two lattes. What's your coffee vice?' If you can hear a mower, comment on that: 'Doesn't the smell of cut grass take you back to being little. I used to live in Scotland on a farm and it reminds me of the summer holidays.' Your immediate environment is ripe with potential conversation.

Gauging Your Listener's Response

Gauging your listener's response is useful in telling how interested they are in you. You can achieve this through a combination of linguistics and body language.

Linguistic clues

Checking the linguistics is a great way to see if somebody wants to chat or flirt more with you, and works equally well in social and work environments. Interpreting linguistic clues is particularly useful if you haven't got the hang of reading body language yet or want another indicator to back it up. The three simple indicators of length, personalising, and questioning give you all the clues you need.

Looking at length

Listening to the length of a response given to a question is your first linguistic clue. If the length of the answer is shorter than the question, this person is either not interested in conversing further or you're going to have to work harder to find a topic they'll be happy to converse on.

If you ask, 'Have you had a good day?' and they respond with a short 'No', they don't want to carry on with this line of questioning and you need to find a new subject. Asking open questions helps to avoid very short answers and facilitates more of a conversation.

If the answer is the same length as your question, for example 'It could've been better', they're not disinterested in conversing with you but you're going to have to do the work.

If the answer is longer than your question, you're leaping up the interested response scale: 'I've had an awful day. Seeing you is the highlight.'

When responding to questions, try to give an answer longer than the question to appear interested in the other person.

Personalising conversation

Personalising is the next clue to look for in a response. 'I', 'me', 'we', and so on are all examples of personalising a response.

In the previous section, 'It could've been better' lacks personalisation and makes telling how interested they are in continuing the conversation harder. In contrast, '*I've* had an awful day. Seeing *you* is the highlight' provides a sign that they're keen to continue talking to you.

Asking questions

Questioning is the final clue you're looking for. Combined with length and personalising, being asked questions yourself is the linguistics jackpot. For example, 'I've had an awful day. Seeing you is the highlight. Was yours any better?'

Going in a positive direction

Gill met Steve at a networking event. She was drawn to him because of his outward confidence and was really pleased she'd made the effort to talk to him, because he was great company. She loved his positive attitude to everything, and it actually drew her attention to the fact that she was constantly putting herself down and was quite negative about work generally. During the conversation, she changed direction and stopped herself from being self-effacing or negative. Changing her attitude took a bit of concentration, but she noticed that when her language altered, Steve became more enthusiastic about her and their discussion. The conversation lasted the rest of the evening. Steve took Gill's card and emailed her a few weeks later to invite her to another event, where the two of them networked like demons and flirted when no one was looking.

Questioning is part of your strategy to expand on your conversation, but can also provide vital clues to let people know you're very interested in continuing talking to them.

Mirroring language

Adding mirroring to the equation helps reinforce your observations. Mirroring is simply copying what the other person is doing and applies to spoken as well as body language. If someone's interested in you, they may mirror anything from the type of language or words that you use to the way you phrase your sentences to your tone of voice. Listen to their responses to see if they adapt any of their language to copy yours.

 Mirroring spoken language is as powerful as copying body language and creates an impact on people on a subconscious level. If you're not great with body language, use mirroring language as your secret weapon. Using the same types and styles of words and language as the other person in your responses immediately increases rapport.

Body language clues

Conversational body language is different to that used in the flirting steps prior to conversation. This type of body language gives an indication of how the other person is responding to you and can be used in both work and social environments.

Eyeing up eye contact

Facial language is very important when you're up close (see Chapter 10 for more on this). Eye contact is the biggest component of facial language and can be very telling. When a person's listening to you they should also be looking at you. Plenty of eye contact and/or increasing eye contact are positive signs.

When a person is attracted to you, their eyes can become wetter, giving the appearance of a twinkle or sparkle.

Research shows that the pupils dilate if a person finds you attractive. As a stand-alone clue, pupil dilation is unreliable, however, as bright lights make the pupils shrink and a dark environment makes them expand.

Expect eye contact to lessen when the other person is speaking and don't interpret it as a negative sign.

Showing the way with their hands

Touching is a way of accentuating a message. When someone likes you, they often touch themselves in a way that draws attention to their vulnerable spots (which we ordinarily protect), such as pulling a chain at the nape of their neck, or that shows where they would like you to be touching them, such as rubbing their arm or thigh or touching their face or lips. The people in Figure 8-1 demonstrate this: the woman by drawing attention to her low-cut neckline and her thigh, and the man by placing his hand near his crotch.

Figure 8-1: Leading with hands.

Leaning in to listen

A person's posture can tell you if they're interested in your conversation. Leaning back in their seat and not looking at you is a clear indication that you're boring them. In contrast, leaning in towards you clearly demonstrates interest.

I beg your pardon?

Abandoning a conversation just because you can't hear it isn't necessary. You can use your body language and proximity to show your interest, which is sometimes more effective and easier than trying to make dazzling conversation.

Mike was at a wedding and was struggling to hear what was being said against the background noise. He kept asking the woman to his left to repeat herself, but still couldn't make out what she was saying. It was seriously impeding the conversation. In the end, Mike just leaned in to listen to her and although he couldn't make out everything that she was saying, he could tell whether it was positive or not by her facial gestures and the inflection in her voice. He managed to laugh in the right places and give the appearance of hanging on her every word. Eventually, Mike asked her if she wanted to go to the lounge for a drink. He was relieved that it was much quieter in the bar and he could actually hear her. They sat on a sofa next to each other and this time she leant in close. Both her words and her intentions were now clear!

Next time you're in a restaurant or bar, observe the postures of the people chatting. Friends mirror each other's posture by leaning in to listen. Can you spot people rowing, or those that aren't interested in each other by their posture alone?

Figure 8-2 illustrates the man's bad listening posture, which is very conversation limiting, and the woman's good listening posture, where the person is keen to hear what the other person is saying.

Figure 8-2: Bad and good listening postures.

Getting your face in gear

Jo wondered why all the people she met seemed to be strange. Despite being attractive and friendly, regular people didn't seem to want anything to do with her. Jo's problem was that nobody had told her face to be friendly. She'd been very shy as a child and had got into the habit of frowning at people she didn't know. She still had that habit twenty years later. Most people were put off speaking to her because her frown stayed in place until she decided if she liked them or not. The odd bods didn't seem to mind if she frowned or not and gravitated towards her. Jo learned to put on a fake smile when she spoke to strangers. It felt odd for her at first, but once she saw the instant effect it had on people, she developed a more natural smile.

Positive facial language and expressions widen your choice of people to talk to and create more meaningful conversations.

Watching for changes in expression

Some people are more animated than others, but being interested in what someone is saying and not changing your expression is actually almost impossible. If someone's hanging on your every word, their facial expressions mirror yours – so avoid frowning! Head nods and tilts, smiling, frowning, eye contact, and blinking are all non-verbal ways of engaging in dialogue, without interrupting the flow of conversation.

Think about the people you find it easy and enjoyable to chat to; they probably all use facial expression to good effect. Now think about people you find it difficult or awkward to converse with; they inevitably use limited facial expressions and/or won't lean in to listen. Be conscious of your own changes in expression during every conversation.

Chapter 9

Being Interesting and Interested

Do you get a tiny pang of jealousy when you see other people effortlessly engage in animated conversation with anyone and everyone they meet? Who wouldn't want to be a conversational whizz? Self-inflicted pressure to appear interesting and make stimulating conversation can be immense, both socially and at work. Reversing this pressure is easy, though; just focus on being interested in the other person. A bit of thought, some research, and a subtle dose of flattery and your conversation will shine.

Showing that You're Interested

Have you ever had a conversation with someone where they've done all the talking and you've just nodded and smiled along politely, only to be told that they've had a really interesting conversation with you and what great company you are? Actually, you've not said a lot but you've looked really interested in what they've said. This, in turn, makes you appear interesting.

Do your research

Knowing in advance who the people are that you're going to be talking to is a massive bonus. Whether you're meeting them in a business or social environment, a vast amount of information exists out there on everyone and the organisations we work for.

Your life as an open book

Stewart was running a girl's name through Google before their first date to find out some more about her so as to have some lines of conversation if things ran dry. Out of curiosity, he ran his own name through and was horrified to see his credit card number and address come up on a fraud site and realise that someone was posing as him on Facebook. Entries he'd contributed to a techie forum also turned up, which was fine, but his responses to a blog that were less than complimentary, he didn't want just anyone to see. Stewart reported the Facebook and credit card fraud, and asked the blogger to remove his posting. After his initial shock, he did manage to find his date's information, the places she'd been on holiday, the music she liked, and an entry in a dating site that even told him her salary bracket.

If you want to keep your life private, use caution when putting things on the net. Letting people find things out about you may, however, attract like-minded people.

The Internet holds the key to getting this information quickly and being able to cross-check sources. Run the person's name through Google to see if anything comes up. Search engines are brilliant for business because you can see if the person's done anything of note or what developments are occurring in their organisations. Social networking sites like Facebook and linkedin get even more traffic than Google, and they're chock-full of information about individuals. With only six degrees of separation between you and every other person on the planet, you'd be surprised who and what you have in common.

Some people may think of research as stalking, but seeking background information is only stalking if you suddenly start telling them information about themselves that they haven't divulged to you!

Just as you're looking up other people, other people will likely look you up too. Identity theft on social networking sites is on the rise. Although such thieves can't hack into your bank account, someone pretending to be you is irritating because you have no control over what they're saying to your friends, for example. If you're not already on Facebook or MySpace, consider at least adding yourself, if for no other reason than to stop anyone else taking your identity and masquerading as you.

Talking about themselves is something most people enjoy. Use the information you gather to steer conversations effortlessly in the right direction and you'll build rapport even faster.

Rapid fire

Jim was meeting Emma for a coffee. He'd found out about the company she worked for and the charity organisation she volunteered with, so he was prepared to demonstrate interest in her. Emma was answering his first question, when he suddenly launched into his second. Out of politeness, she abandoned her response to the first question and started answering the second. Again, Jim interrupted with another question, and so it continued. Emma found his constant interrupting annoying and felt he just wasn't interested in anything she was saying as he was constantly changing the subject. Emma eventually challenged Jim and he apologised profusely; he hadn't realised he was creating this impression. On their next date, Jim followed the three simple conventions and everything went smoothly.

How many questions you ask isn't what makes for interesting conversation; the flow of the dialogue is what matters. Use the three rules to keep things ticking over smoothly.

Follow convention

Certain conventions need to be observed when trying to appear interested whilst making conversation. Follow these three simple conventions in any kind of conversation, from dealing with clients to flirting at parties, and watch your relationships improve:

- ✔ **Don't ask more than one question at once.** Not only does doing so waste your material, you confuse the other person and the conversation will be shorter as a result.

- ✔ **Let the person answer the question.** Nothing is more irritating than someone answering their own question or trying to put words into your mouth.

    Whilst listening to their responses, watch their faces too. Any subject that elicits a long answer and an animated expression is a thread worth pursuing further, especially if you can add a similar anecdote of your own. (Head to Chapter 8 for information on personal disclosure.)

    When telling of a similar experience, make sure you don't outdo their story; doing so's an instant rapport killer. If you haven't got a similar experience to share, ask them about the details of the story to add colour and dimension to it.

- ✔ **Don't talk at tangents.** Following on from the theme of their conversation shows your interest; darting off at tangents may make you look like you're incapable of holding a conversation or you're not interested in what they're saying.

Being polite and following convention makes conversation flow much easier. Having a long, gentle conversation is so much better than a series of brilliant one-liners that don't go any further. Chapter 8 offers tips on how to converse successfully.

Listen more, speak less

Teachers often tell pupils they have two ears and only one mouth and they should use them in that proportion. This advice also applies to making conversation. If you're not listening to what the other person is saying, you won't know how to respond or where to move the conversation to next.

Novice TV presenters often seem to fire out set questions without taking into account great opportunities to expand on interviewees' answers. Practised interviewers, in contrast, seem to effortlessly link one subject to the next by really listening to interviewees' responses.

If you're doing more talking than listening when you meet someone for the first time, you're talking too much.

Tailor what you say

Research shows that men are more factually orientated and women are more emotionally driven. Salespeople know this, and often use different strategies for selling the same product to different sexes. In any discourse, though, someone is buying and someone is selling, and you need to bear this in mind when thinking of lines of conversation. Knowing what men and women tend to focus on in conversations can help you tailor what you say to the person you're speaking with.

Making conversation takes two, so don't feel the talking's all your responsibility. Being prepared, however, makes you feel more confident that you won't run out of things to say, which in itself keeps the conversation buoyant. Check out Chapter 8 for tips on good topics to chat about.

Becoming More Interesting

You might assume that to become more interesting you'd need some dazzling conversation on your part. However, you can easily become more interesting to other people simply by focusing on the other person – both on the words they use and the body language they demonstrate. The key to being perceived as interesting yourself is actually to just be interested in what the other person is saying. By demonstrating interest in the other person, you present yourself to them as an engaging, thoughtful, and enjoyable person to converse with. That makes you more interesting to them and, in turn, makes them keen to find out more about you.

Copying is the highest form of flattery and one of the fastest ways to become more interesting without too much effort.

Recognising the patterns of a conversation

A conversation has a pattern to it, which varies depending on who you're talking to. For example, conversations with your granny may be quite slow, and you know that when she starts telling you one of her stories nothing will interrupt her until she's finished. With your best friend, conversation may be fast and animated, and with your boss, calm and measured.

Following the conversation as it progresses

When you strike up a conversation with someone, and it goes well, the conversation moves through several different stages. In fact, making conversation with someone you're trying to get to know is a bit like dancing to music at a wedding. First come the same old tunes that everyone knows and which get you in the mood. Next, as the atmosphere hots up, you find the people who like the tracks you like and get on down to those. Finally, you hit the smoochy numbers and the partner you've got to know over the evening is suddenly up close and personal. If the music jumped from classical to jazz to hip hop, you wouldn't know if you were coming or going and the dancing wouldn't last very long. The same goes for your lines of conversation.

Being positive

Language makes a big difference to how you view something. Choose your words carefully and you're more interesting to the people you want to impress. Being positive is absolutely crucial.

Talking positively helps you maintain an open posture, an attractive tone of voice, and an animated and attractive facial expression – see Figure 9-1. Negative language will close your posture – you may find your arms and/or legs start crossing – and the quality of your voice will suffer. You start to close the conversation down.

Figure 9-1: Positive posture.

Positive language has a huge effect on the people you're speaking to. They feel energised around you and want to further the conversation. You'll be a magnet for other conversations in the room, too.

 Make a list of all the negative words and phrases you routinely use and work out positive replacements. See how much better you feel generally after only a couple of days of ditching the negatives. Table 9-1 lists some positive alternatives to the negative phrases you may find yourself saying.

No problems here

I leased a car recently and everything that could go wrong with it, did. Every time I rang the agency, the man was sweetness and light, and convinced it would all be sorted soon. After a couple of calls, I noticed that he never used the word 'problem', even though I was suffering from many of them thanks to his organisation. He only had challenges'. Eventually, every time I heard him use the phrase, 'It's a bit of a challenge, but we'll fix it', I laughed. I liked his positive approach to things and have banned the word 'problem' from my vocabulary. My life is now full of little challenges and they're much nicer to conquer than problems are to solve.

Table 9-1	Positive Alternatives
Replace This	*With This*
I'm dreading this	I can't wait to try
I had a dreadful journey here	It was an unusual but eventful trip
I'm useless	I'll get it right next time
I'm bored	Let's find something more fun to do
I hate that	I'm gradually acquiring the taste for
This is a problem	I'm working on a challenge

 Avoid putting yourself down at the end of sentences; doing so's unattractive and boring.

Making People Feel Important

Feeling special is something nobody refuses. Making people feel significant is especially important in relation to flirting, developing new friendships, and success at work. Fortunately, you use exactly the same skills in all these contexts to a greater or lesser extent. The next three sections offer strategies you can use to make others feel important; the last section tells you how to make colleagues, friends, and people you're interested in feel important.

Mirroring their language

Copying a person's language is a great way to build rapport. Just listen for words or phrases that stand out in the conversation and also use them. If they refer to their dog as their 'doggie', using doggie in your response sounds familiar and will endear you to them faster than if you refer to their beloved pet as 'the dog'.

If they're the type of person who 'loves' to do this and 'loves' to do that, they're clearly a passionate person. By adopting the same or similar approach in your choice of words, you bond much quicker.

For more information on using linguistics to determine how interested someone is in you, see Chapter 8.

Copycats

It was a blustery summer's day in what had otherwise been a damp squib of a summer. As they walked along the beach, Patsy turned to her friend to comment on the nice day. 'Those clouds have heavy bottoms, I think it could be rain on the way,' responded Elizabeth. Patsy was disappointed in the response. 'You're always being so negative, why can't you have something positive to say for once?' she berated her friend. Elizabeth wasn't trying to be negative; she'd just happened to notice the clouds exactly when Patsy was commenting on the nice day and was effectively thinking out loud. Elizabeth was careful afterwards to avoid mentioning anything that could be misconstrued as negative.

To develop the best rapport, use the tone and style of language of the person you're conversing with.

Next time you have a conversation with a good friend, listen for common words and phrases that you both use. You may also find that you adopt the same attitudes in your conversations, for example being positive or negative or sitting on the fence.

Letting them take the floor

People generally love the sound of their own voices and talking about themselves; after all, it's a subject they know well.

If you give the other person enough space, they'll generally find the words to fill it. This strategy serves two purposes: not only do you get to find out lots about the person you're talking to, which helps you build more rapport, it also leads the other person to believe that you're fascinated by them, which is a very flattering notion.

As well as being a great social strategy, letting others do the talking works well in the office too.

When making conversation, don't be afraid to give people the space to answer; the more space they have, the more they reveal themselves to you.

Putting it into action

To start capitalising on your skills, you need to put them into action – in your workplace, to make new friends, and get more dates. That's where this section comes in.

Boss's pet

Whenever Gemma fancied a lazy afternoon, she'd casually drop a question into the conversation about one of her boss's pet subjects. This generally initiated a two-hour monologue, interspersed with tea and chocolate biscuits, which he'd happily supply in return for the opportunity to talk about his youth in Norway and his time as a professional footballer. Gemma was genuinely quite interested in her boss, but she also enjoyed slacking off work into the bargain.

As hard as her colleague Graham tried, he couldn't figure out Gemma's success in getting their boss off the subject of work and having a skive, but then Graham wasn't a big fan of listening or letting anyone else do the talking.

If you're looking for an easy conversation, discover the other person's main passion and let them run with it.

Enhancing your career

Practising in the office is a great way to hone your skills before you let them loose on the person of your desires. You'll be pleasantly surprised by the results and may even get a pay rise or promotion into the bargain.

To make people feel important, try these strategies:

- ✔ Make a point of taking the initiative because it makes the other person feel pleased that you made the effort to approach them.
- ✔ Greet everyone you meet with a cheery hello to gain a reputation for being friendly.
- ✔ When someone speaks, nod in agreement while you listen – they'll talk for up to three times longer.
- ✔ Smile – lots!
- ✔ In meetings, if someone is quiet, ask for their opinion – you'll appear consultative and inclusive.
- ✔ If someone says something you agree with, say so.
- ✔ Pay genuine compliments freely.
- ✔ Thank your boss for their help and guidance.
- ✔ Volunteer to do the things that other people don't want to – but not all the time.

Too clever by half

Ian was a bright chap and didn't tolerate fools gladly. Unfortunately, he considered most of the people he worked with to fall into that category. In meetings, he'd create an austere impression by leaning back in his chair and looking down his nose when other people were speaking. When anyone challenged what he said, he'd verbally beat them into the ground. Ian's problem wasn't so much what he said but how he said it: he made his colleagues feel like idiots.

Ian's boss finally took him to one side and told him to address his behaviour towards other people. Instead of interrupting them to tell them they were wrong, he should let people talk and then respond in a non-aggressive manner. Initially, Ian didn't like this approach because meetings took much longer. He still got the outcome he wanted, though, and he was still very unpopular in meetings. His boss told Ian to stick with his new approach; change takes time to stick. Eventually people started to respond to Ian differently; they listened when he persuaded them his way was better, and usually agreed, and his boss observed his greater respect for others and offered him promotion.

Sometimes, doing things differently can seem futile if you achieve the same result. Making people feel good about themselves and as though they've been listened to and appreciated, however, will win you more than just brownie points. Be patient; a change in attitude takes time to sink in. Stick with the changes you make in your own behaviour until you get the response you want.

Cultivating more friends

Finding friends becomes harder as you get older. Opportunities don't present themselves the way they did when you were at school or college. People who play team sports have the greatest opportunities to meet new people, but if you're a working lone parent who's relocated from your home town, life can be quite lonely. Using all your lovely flirting skills on new people not only wins them over, it also prepares you for when you're ready to dazzle Mr or Miss Right. Only one rule of thumb exists when looking for new friends: if they're breathing, they're a possible friend!

To cultivate new friends, follow this advice:

✓ Take opportunities to speak to new people, greeting them with a smile and maintaining a happy demeanour.

✓ Be interested in what they have to say and ask them for their thoughts, even if the subject's not something you're interested in.

✓ Nod gently in agreement when the other person is talking.

Billy no mates

Victoria's kids were both at school and lots of the other mums had gone back to work. She was feeling quite lonely and didn't feel she had the opportunity to meet new people. Actually, she met lots of people in the course of a day: fellow dog walkers, members of the gym, and other mums at the school gates. But then Victoria took the initiative and followed the cultivating friends strategy. She started to speak to some of the older dog walkers who weren't in so much of a rush and discovered that they were good company. The age gap was irrelevant and she began looking forward to their walks together. At the gym, Victoria started chatting to a woman who returned her smile and within a couple of weeks they were meeting regularly for coffee. She spoke to the new mums at school and suggested a small group of them got together for a drink once a week. Gradually the children got to know each other too and the mums and kids started meeting up at weekends. Having so many new friends meant Victoria didn't have to rely so heavily on her long-standing ones and could even gently ditch one whose friendship she'd outgrown.

Taking the initiative to meet other people and be interested in them can feel awkward at first. Once you've got the hang of it, though, you'll never lose it.

✔ Compliment them.

✔ Don't be in a rush to get away and let them know you look forward to bumping into them again.

Boosting your flirting prowess

Making someone feel important when you're flirting with them is very easy, especially if the other person finds you attractive. Even if the other person doesn't realise they're attracted to you yet, by following the advice in this section you'll boost their ego so much and make them feel so special they'll naturally feel warmer towards you.

Making someone feel as though they're the centre of your universe, even if only for the duration of a conversation, is a powerful strategy. Remain quiet whilst they talk, don't interrupt, and always respond with a personal experience of the subject they've just talked on. As you do so, remember to:

✔ Smile

✔ Gaze into their eyes

✔ Nod when they're speaking

✔ Agree with what they've said

✔ Flatter, flatter, flatter

Treating 'em mean doesn't keep 'em keen

Visiting friends, Nigel was pleasantly surprised to be introduced to Sally. He was polite at first but, as he became more comfortable, suddenly started offering back-handed compliments that verged on rude. Sally had no idea what she'd done to offend him. When Sally popped to the bathroom, the host asked Nigel why he was being such an idiot. Nigel had thought his flirtation was going very well and was oblivious to the offence he was causing; to him, his comments were just playful banter. 'That sort of thing might impress the guys in the rugby team, but it won't work on women.' chastised the host. Nigel turned tack and spent the rest of the evening being nice to Sally, listening to what she had to say, agreeing with the points she was making, hanging on her every word, and paying her compliments. Although Sally was confused at first, she did eventually fall for his charms.

Putting people down, even in jest, won't impress anyone. Play nice and make them feel important if you want to win them over.

You may feel this approach is too obvious – but it works!

 Resting your hand *against* your face gives the appearance of being interested, but don't rest your face *on* your hand as doing so indicates boredom and disinterest – Figure 9-2 demonstrates the difference. Women are more likely to adopt this pose than men. Men will usually lean more into the woman's territory by putting their arm across the table or on the back of her chair.

Figure 9-2: Fascinated woman (left); bored woman (right).

 People respond more positively to smiles, but grinning like a Cheshire cat isn't necessary. Adopting a slight, closed-lip smile, with the corners of your mouth turning up just enough to make your cheeks raise slightly and the corners of your eye crinkle, makes you a more attractive listener.

The merry widow

Jane was a widow, with no plans to find a new husband – but she was never short of offers. The men loved her. When her friends watched what she was doing, it was actually very simple. She gazed at the person speaking to her, and smiled broadly whenever they said something amusing. She was also free with her compliments, smattering the conversation with 'You're so clever', 'You're so funny', and so on. It was a simple, but brilliant and unintentional, strategy. Jane was a natural flirt.

The simplest solutions, designed by Mother Nature, are often the best; look friendly, be interested, make them feel special, and you boost your flirting prowess with very little effort.

Using Compliments Well

Compliments are universally accepted vehicles for letting people know you like them or some particular thing about them. Nothing is more reassuring and confidence boosting than receiving a genuine compliment. Many people aren't keen on paying compliments because they feel that doing so shows their hand and makes them feel more vulnerable to rejection. Giving compliments doesn't weaken your position, however. In fact, one complimentary sentence can consolidate it.

If everyone made a point of paying a couple of compliments a day, the world would be a much friendlier and happier place. Consider how often you've felt negatively towards someone but changed your mind when they've said nice things about you.

You can compliment people on everything from the way they do their job, to how they treat you, to how they look. You have no excuse not to get the compliment habit.

Knowing how to receive a compliment is also an art in itself. Fumbling an acceptance could be enough to ensure you don't receive another one from that person, and rejecting a compliment is rude and insulting to the compliment giver. Coyness and self-effacement show a lack of confidence; accepting graciously allows it to have maximum impact.

Making the perfect compliment

Opening or chat-up lines don't have to be contrived and neither do compliments. If you're not used to paying them, stick to something simple.

Apparently, the words 'you' and 'nice' feature most commonly in compliments, so obviously the phrase 'You look nice' works perfectly well.

Paying genuine compliments is important. If you don't believe what you're saying, the other person will know. Also, if you feel a little embarrassed about giving compliments, avoid comedy facial expressions such as raising an eyebrow, nodding, or winking; not unsurprisingly, they may be viewed as insincere and have the opposite effect from the one you intended.

Complimenting women

Generally, women invest a fair amount of time in their appearance, taking care with everything from their hair to make-up and clothes. If you can see that a woman has made an effort with or a change to her appearance, complimenting her specifically on this works more effectively than offering more general compliments. And compliments don't need to be limited to the opposite sex. If your boss, neighbour, friend, or just someone you see regularly in the street looks nice, tell them.

Complimenting men

Men are generally much better at accepting compliments than women, but they don't receive as many. If you compliment a man, therefore, he's much more likely to notice you. Men appreciate compliments relating to a greater variety of things, too: personal possessions, favourite sporting team, physical appearance. Try to compliment them on something you're interested in too to get the conversation started.

I always compliment a man who smells good, and they always seem surprised that I've noticed. Try 'That aftershave smells great; what is it?' to initiate a debate on your favourite aromas.

Complimenting colleagues

A myriad of untapped complimenting opportunities are available in the office. Rather than concerning the way someone looks they tend more towards a person's professional conduct and their relationships in the office. People genuinely want to know they're doing a good job and that they're valued, whether you fancy them or just view them as a colleague. Try any of the compliment openers below to put some zing into your relationships with your boss, colleagues, suppliers, and clients:

- ✔ 'I really like the way you . . .'
- ✔ 'Where would we be without your help with . . .'
- ✔ 'I'd really respect your opinion on . . .'

Red neck flapper

Tori had just started work in a new office. She was a little shy, but was putting on a confident front and it seemed to be working. Until, that is, a guy she liked in the office next door complimented her on her new haircut. She stared at the floor, flapped and babbled, said it was very ordinary (even though she really liked it herself), and eventually flushed bright red. The conversation ground to a dead halt. 'I'm sorry, I didn't mean to embarrass you,' offered the poor guy, as he crept away feeling awkward for unsettling her.

Tori could've kicked herself. She practised giving herself compliments and receiving them with a simple 'Thank you'. She was ready for the next time he said something nice. Weeks went by and he never offered her another word. Then he had a haircut, and she thought she'd repay the compliment. He accepted it with a smile, they chatted some more and he offered to buy her a coffee.

Complimenting friends

Friends are the best people to practise compliments on because they know you have no hidden agenda and appreciate the gesture. Receiving a compliment from someone you know and trust carries far more weight than one from a stranger. Make a point of complimenting your friends on something different every time you see them.

Try 'I'm really glad to have you as a mate' or 'Chatting to you really brightens my day'.

Accepting compliments graciously

Learning to accept compliments is crucial in the flirting game. If you ignore a compliment or get very embarrassed when you're on the receiving end of one, the person you're with is unlikely to pay you another, and you may even embarrass them in the process. A simple 'Thank you', whilst you look them in the eye, is sufficient to accept a compliment.

Responding to a compliment on your outfit with, 'This old thing, I've just dragged it out from the back of my wardrobe', means you ruin the person's attempt to ingratiate themselves with you. Now you have to work doubly hard to get your flirtation back on track.

Being coy isn't a solution to receiving a compliment either. Coyness displays a lack of confidence, and if you're a flusher, you'll end up red.

Never reject a compliment, because it can be interpreted as a rejection of the person who offered it. Have a simple response ready and accept compliments with a smile and good eye contact to help your flirtation along.

Part III

Developing Killer Rapport with Body Language

The 5th Wave   By Rich Tennant

"I don't know a lot about body language, but I think that guy over there wants you to approach him."

In this part . . .

This part helps you get to grips with body language. You can find out how to send the right signals to get you noticed and how to read the signs coming back your way. I also cover all the secret flirting skills used by men and women to increase your flirting prowess.

Chapter 10

Giving Off the Right Signals

. . . .

In This Chapter

▶ Taking a closer look at body language

▶ Getting to grips with personal space

▶ Mastering facial language

▶ Gesturing with flirtatious fingers

▶ Being provocative

. . . .

*F*lirting is mostly non-verbal – your body is literally doing the talking. Believe it or not, your body language, appearance, and tone of voice have an even bigger impact on the impression you make than your words. The big question is: are you aware of your non-verbal abilities? How are you perceived in your everyday communications: meetings, one-to-one conversations, presentations, and flirtations? Does your non-verbal communication enhance your message or detract from it?

This chapter is all about you giving off the right signals to whomever you wish to flirt with. In Chapter 11, you can find what you need to build on this and to be aware of the signals and clues you're looking for in the other person to progress your flirtation. To know more about how women and men differ in their flirting, check out Chapter 12.

Looking at the Importance of Body Language

After you've said and done all the right things, your body and facial language do the rest of the work and give you all the clues you need to tell whether you're being flirted with or to let someone know how you feel about them without actually having to say a word.

Body language and first impressions

As Figure 10-1 shows, your body language, appearance, and tone of voice form over 90 per cent of a first impression. The words account for a meagre 7 per cent of the impact. Yet, if you're like most people, you probably spend more time worrying about your words than you do about the delivery or non-verbal communication you make.

Figure 10-1 makes clear that the areas with the largest proportions need the most attention to create the greatest impact. A radical change to improve your flirting abilities is obviously called for!

Up to 21 meetings may be necessary for someone to change their first impression of you. You may not get the chance to meet them another 21 times, so make the right impression first time round.

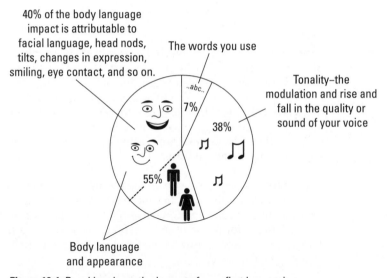

40% of the body language impact is attributable to facial language, head nods, tilts, changes in expression, smiling, eye contact, and so on.

The words you use

Tonality–the modulation and rise and fall in the quality or sound of your voice

..abc..

7%

38%

55%

Body language and appearance

Figure 10-1: Breaking down the impact of your first impression.

The impact of body language

Not only do you have to give off the right signs – such as good eye contact, great posture and proximity, smiling, and so on – to create a positive impact, you also have to be able to read and interpret body language. Reading others' body language is vital to flirting, socialising, and business success.

The ostrich approach to flirting

Khan worked in IT, in a male-dominated environment. He wasn't great with the opposite sex, so went and bought himself a book by a renowned lothario, learned it verbatim, and set about applying the rules meticulously. His success rate was zero, with the added embarrassment of the odd slap and being ejected by a doorman. What Khan had failed to appreciate is that it takes two to flirt; you can't just flirt at someone and hope it works. Fortunately, Khan then came across a book on body language. Not only did he discover that he could actually see what was going on with someone else, he also realised that he could influence the situation by adapting his own body language. He practised reading the people at work. He gave up communicating by email and actually went to colleagues' desks to ask them questions and gauge their responses from their actions. Finally, he used his new-found body language skills on women and to his surprise discovered he didn't need a set of cheesy chat-up lines.

To keep your flirtations on track, make sure that you not only use good body language but also check the responses of others.

 How adept are your skills? To find out, while you're sitting in meetings or at the dinner table, observe the body language of the people around you. Try to determine who likes or dislikes each other, who's having a secret affair, who are the most and least dominant in the room, and who are the most and least likely to be interrupted? Just by becoming interested in people and their behaviour, you open up a whole new world of clues right under your nose.

You can find out more about reading and interpreting body language in Chapter 11.

Getting Your Proximity Right

Understanding how to position yourself in relation to other people is a vital skill. Proximity can make or break an encounter. Too far away and they lose interest due to the lack of connection, too close and you frighten them off as you're encroaching on their space.

 Using the right body language, but in the wrong proximity or part of the flirting process, can be fatal. The following sections explain how to get exactly where you want to be and what you should be doing when you get there.

Finding the right proximity

Everyone operates in their own territory or personal space, which is basically the bubble of air we get used to having between ourselves and others. Although studies can give a general guide to how large these areas are (explained in the following list and shown in Figure 10-2), you need to watch the individual you're connecting with for subtle clues as to how much theirs differs to the general rule. Also keep in mind that these distances tend to increase between two men and reduce between two women:

- ✔ **The public zone:** 3.6 metres plus. This is the comfortable distance to stand when addressing a large group of people.

- ✔ **The social zone:** Between 1.22–3.6 metres. You stand at this distance from strangers or tradespeople visiting your home, people you don't know very well, or new people at work.

- ✔ **The personal zone:** Between 0.46–1.22 metres. This is the distance you stand from people at office parties, social functions, and family gatherings.

- ✔ **The intimate zone:** Between 15–45 centimetres. You have to take care when entering this zone as people guard it like private property. Only people who are emotionally close to you, such as children, parents, partner, close friends, lovers, and pets can be this proximate.

- ✔ **The close intimate zone:** 15 centimetres from the body. This area can only be entered during intimate physical contact.

The size of your personal space is dependent on the density of the population where you grew up and where you currently live. People from places like Japan are used to crowding and therefore think nothing of standing right next to someone on an empty train platform. People brought up in the country, in contrast, are used to enjoying much larger personal space.

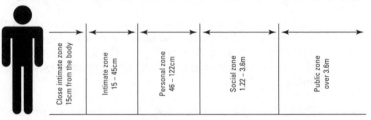

Figure 10-2: Personal zone distances.

Too close for comfort

Jess was making an effort to make new friends at the local gym. She got friendly with one of the instructors, but found it difficult to be around her as the friendlier the instructor became, the closer she liked to get. Jess would find herself bobbing backward when she got too close, then taking a step back; unfortunately, the instructor would immediately take a step forward to close the gap. Ultimately, Jess only felt comfortable speaking to her with a table between them so she couldn't get too close, which meant Jess wouldn't go out for drinks when invited and missed out on the social life she craved. Jess tried to adjust her personal space so she wasn't so uncomfortable around the instructor, and when she got to know her a bit better she asked why she always stood so close. The instructor had no idea that she was encroaching on her personal space, as she was used to being in cramped aerobics studios and standing in close proximity was quite normal for her. They made a lighthearted agreement that the instructor would look out for Jess bobbing and not get so close, and that Jess would give her a poke if she wasn't getting the message. Jess's new friendship has opened up all sorts of new relationships to her, which she wouldn't have access to if she hadn't dealt with the proximity issue.

Get to grips with your personal space and be mindful of others' to get your relationships running smoothly.

Another exception to the distance/intimacy rules is when the special gap is based on social status. You could be best buddies with your boss or somebody senior at work, for example playing football together, and then socialise in each other's personal or intimate zone; however, at work, your boss may keep you at the social zone distance in order to maintain the unwritten social status rules.

You can tell when you're too close to someone because they'll initially bob or lean backwards when you enter their space. This is the briefest of movements and you need to look out for it or you may miss it. They may continue to tolerate you in their space or you could find them angling away from you. If this is the case, move away from them until they're comfortable.

Closing the gap between you

Progressing your flirtation involves closing the gap between you. That doesn't mean shuffling right up close to them on a seat or at a bar, but rather by leaning or angling your upper body in. In Figure 10-3 you can see how the couple has closed the gap between them, not by sitting together, but by leaning in towards each other. Their hips are clearly much farther apart than their shoulders, but you can tell they're enjoying a flirtation by the leaning together spacing of their torsos.

This move also works well when making new friends; close the gap to make them feel closer to you.

Figure 10-3: Closing the gap between you.

Making the situation more intimate

How far their hips are apart when embracing reveals the relationship between two people. If you're hugging a close relative or friend, your hips are at least 6 inches away from theirs. In contrast, if you're embracing someone you're intimately involved with, you do a full body torso press and move within the close intimate zone.

To make the situation more intimate you need to either invite them into your space or start to invade theirs. (See Chapter 11 for more on inviting someone into your space.)

You can see from Figure 10-4 that the man and woman have placed their glasses at the edge of their territory, but she has extended her reach into his territory and he has happily let her; they're both still smiling and maintaining eye contact. If he wasn't comfortable with her moving closer, he'd be pulling back and making the gap between them larger. Their hips are still well apart but their heads are as close as they can be with the table between them and they're touching – this flirtation is progressing nicely.

Figure 10-4: Getting more intimate.

Cracking the Facial Language Code

Making sense of body language can seem a bit daunting if you're not used to it. A good place to start is to focus on your facial language, because the face is the area that people pay the most attention to when they're in conversation.

Facial language consists of head nods, tilts, blinks, winks, changes in expression, smiles, and eye contact. The more animated your expression, the easier it is for people to read your mood and intentions.

Studies have shown that facial language counts for around 40 per cent of the impact of your body language. The farther away things are from the brain, the harder they are to control, but as the face is right up there, you should be able to exert a reasonable level of control over it, to give the impression you desire.

The seven expressions

People can gain a great deal of information about your emotional state from the expressions on your face. The attitudes you convey, or are being conveyed towards you, can be clearly seen.

Whilst dozens of descriptions for facial expressions exist – delirious, ecstatic, devastated, and so on – actually only seven facial expressions can accurately be identified. Anything else is just interpretation and thus can be misinterpreted.

The seven emotional expressions are:

- ✔ Fear
- ✔ Anger
- ✔ Interest
- ✔ Contempt
- ✔ Disgust
- ✔ Happiness
- ✔ Sadness

 The face is usually the first part of a person we look at. Adopting a positive expression, using good eye contact and a smile, is a powerful means of communication with both the object of your desire and your colleagues. Remember, if someone thinks you like them, they're much more likely to like you in return.

 Research shows that people with attractive faces are often credited with having a number of other attributes, like honesty and intellect, which they may not possess! Don't assume that someone who is very attractive is perfect.

 Be conscious of what your face is doing both at work (for practice) and when you're socialising, to get used to using the full range of facial expressions available to you. Try nodding when someone is speaking; research shows that by nodding, you appear more engaged and interested and they're likely to speak for up to three times longer.

The power of the gaze

Apparently, the eyes are the window to the soul and you can tell a lot about what someone is thinking by where and how they're looking. Humans are the only primates to have developed the whites of the eye as an aid to communication. The whites allow others to see where you're looking, and the direction in which you look is linked to your emotional state. If you look down and to your right, you're likely to be recalling a feeling; down and to the left and you're most likely to be talking internally to yourself.

Research shows that to build a good rapport with someone, your gaze should meet theirs between 60 to 70 per cent of the time during conversation. If someone observes you looking at them a lot, they're likely to think you like them and in return are more likely to like you.

Here's an interesting titbit: research also shows that both sexes have a greater ability to read eye signals than body signals, and that women are better at it than men.

You can use your eyes to convey other messages and engender other reactions as well:

- ✔ Ladies, widen your eyes by raising your eyebrows and eyelids to create a baby-faced look. This look has a powerful effect on men: it releases hormones in their brain and stimulates the desire to protect and defend females.

  Princess Diana made looking coy an art form, eliciting maternal and paternal reactions towards her from the public. Lowering the head and looking up is not only a submissive gesture, it appeals to men because it makes the woman appear more child-like and vulnerable. You can see in Figure 10-5 that the woman has lowered her head and is giving a sideways glance in a submissive pose, which men find attractive.

- ✔ Guys, if trimming your eyebrows, trim them from the top of the eyebrow down to make your eyes appear narrower and more authoritative.

Figure 10-5: Looking coy and submissive.

Hooked in four seconds

A TV presenter found herself single and keen to find a new man, but was having little success. She followed the four-second rule just as a laugh, and was astonished at how well it worked. Not only was it painless and rejection free, it had the men flocking over to say hello without her having to do anything. She said she felt quite cheesy the first time she tried it, but after a couple of goes, she loved the simplicity and efficacy of the approach.

Try this really easy, obvious tip at the first opportunity. You'll be amazed at how easy doing the four-second glance is – it will become a staple trick in your flirting armoury.

The four-second glance

Four seconds doesn't seem long when you say it, but can seem like forever the first time you actively try to stare at someone for this long. The four-second glance is:

- ✔ Really simple to do
- ✔ Highly effective in getting someone to spot that you've noticed them
- ✔ The first step in the non-verbal hello process
- ✔ Virtually rejection risk free

Body language that stands out from the norm is more eye-catching. If you're looking around as usual, how can you let someone know you're actually checking them out and liking what you see, without actually speaking to them?

The four-second glance is as straightforward as it sounds:

1. **Look at the person for four seconds.**
2. **Look away briefly.**
3. **Look back.**

    If they're still looking, take it as a positive sign that they've noticed your four-second glance and are checking you out.

A four-second glance is long enough to let someone know you've noticed them. Avoid staring for longer than that – a ten-second glance indicates that you're about to either beat them up or leap into bed with them!

What's in a smile?

Smiling is very important. It not only lets people know you like them, this facial expression is also universally considered to show happiness. Smiling is also a submission signal, which means people aren't likely to feel threatened around you when you do it. Smiling should be a well-used part of your flirting armoury.

Smile regularly, even if you don't feel like it, because doing so directly influences other people's attitudes and how they respond to you. Smiling is contagious; it causes someone to smile back at you even if your smile is fake and so is theirs.

Fake or real? Judging smiles

The smile is controlled by two sets of muscles, one that runs down the side of the face and connects with the mouth, and one that pulls the eyes back. You can consciously control the muscles of your mouth, which means you can fake a smile, but the muscles that control the eyes act independently and can't be faked. Check the sincerity of a smile by looking for wrinkles around the eyes. Not surprisingly, insincere people smile only with their mouths and it's a turn off for the recipient. Figure 10-6 demonstrates both a fake smile and a real one.

Here's a smile check you can use to see whether the smiles you're getting back are real or polite false ones. Sometimes people can fake a smile so hard that lines do appear around their eyes, but this effect is actually caused by their cheeks bunching up. As an extra check, the eye cover fold (the fleshy part between the eyelid and the eyebrow) moves downward and the ends of the eyebrows dip slightly in a genuine smile.

Figure 10-6: A fake smile (left); a real smile (right).

Space invader

Sally was on a blind date with Angus and they were sitting opposite each other at the table. The waiter gave them both a menu and left them to consider their orders. Whilst she was choosing, Angus pushed his knife and fork out to the side, his glass forward, and the salt and pepper over the middle of the small table onto Sally's side. Finally, he 'cornered' Sally on a small piece of the table with his cutlery and glass. She obviously felt invaded and set about trying to recapture her half of the table. Angus paid Sally compliments but she was too distracted by now to notice. Angus had made a terrible mistake; he'd aggressively dominated the table before he got to know Sally and had put her on the defensive.

Sally playfully challenged Angus and asked him why he felt the need to dominate her half of the table. He laughed and said he hadn't even realised he'd done it. This probably explained why none of his previous dates had seemed keen to meet again.

On the next date, Angus kept his hands off the cutlery and the lunch started much more positively – in fact, they got on like a house on fire. After the main course, Sally cleared the condiments away from the middle to the edge of the table, then pushed her glass over onto his side, leaving a clear gap between them. Angus reached out across the table and offered her his hand to hold. Sealed with a nice bit of intentional touching, they enjoyed a lovely romantic lunch.

Use the contents of your table, or whatever is in your space, to open up a gap between you and invite the other person into your territory to take your flirting to the next level without having to say a word.

Common smile types

Other than the straightforward toothy smile we all acknowledge as friendly and welcoming, you need to be aware of a number of other smiles:

- **Tight-lipped:** Where the lips are drawn across the face to form a straight line and no teeth are visible. This smile's common in people who don't want to reveal that they don't like someone, or that they're holding back their feelings.

- **Twisted:** Where the smile isn't symmetrical. This expression is deliberate and is intended to convey sarcasm.

- **Dropped jaw:** This smile conveys the impression that the person is laughing or playful.

- **Coy:** A smile combined with looking up sideways, as perfected by Princess Diana. The smiler looks playful and seductive and is conveying a definite flirting signal.

Practise recognising these common types of smile to identify what responses your smiles are eliciting and who's flirting with you.

Letting Your Fingers Do the Talking

So much can be said without ever uttering a word. These days we rely heavily on text, email, and instant messaging to do the talking for us, but if someone you're having a drink with receives a text from you saying 'touch me', they'll be thrown, alarmed, and probably uncooperative. Sometimes only your fingers can do the talking.

Taking over your space and theirs

When you first start flirting with someone you're both in your own little territory, but when things start to get more intimate you need to start invading their space, in the nicest possible sense, or inviting them into yours.

Anything on a surface near you can be used as a non-verbal invitation. By clearing things out of the way, you literally clear a path to you. By pushing your objects (wine glass, bag, napkin) into their space, you test if they're receptive to the next move being made.

Look at Figure 10-7. Can you tell who's invading whose space? They've met in the middle with their glasses; he's holding his position by holding his glass and using his arm as a barrier and she's doing the running. She's ventured into his space with a reassuring intentional touch on the arm and you can tell by his smile that he's happily accepted the move and their flirtation has just moved up a gear.

Figure 10-7: She's venturing into his space.

When you're next eating with friends, family, or colleagues, experiment with the position of items on the table to redefine your territory and see how they react. Your boss probably won't be happy about you invading her space, but your best friend probably won't mind.

Getting in touch with yourself

Touching yourself is a subtle way of conveying that you're interested in the other person and you'd like to invite them to flirt more with you. By touching yourself you draw attention to your body and to those parts where you'd like the other person to touch you.

Touching yourself can also be very reassuring and calming if you're feeling uncomfortable.

In Figure 10-8, the woman is touching herself to draw the man's attention to her cleavage.

Keep your self-touching to the upper part of your body for maximum effect. Watching someone vigorously rubbing their thighs in anticipation can be quite off-putting! However, a seductive stroke with the tips of your fingers can be quite appealing.

Figure 10-8: Attention goes to the location you're touching.

Intentional touching

Touch has a long-lasting and positive physiological effect. When someone has received bad news, you may automatically feel the need to put your arms around them to comfort them and protect them from the hurt. Yet in the highly litigious environment in which we live, touching has become almost taboo. Used appropriately and at the right time, however, touching can really cement a flirtation and move things along to the next level.

You probably do more intentional touching than you're aware of. It can be a split-second action, which is usually over before you know it, but the effect lasts.

When touching someone else, you have to first make sure that your proximity is appropriate (see the earlier section 'Getting Your Proximity Right') and that the touch is justified; that is, you have a good reason to touch them: they've just told you a joke, you're agreeing with them on something, you're showing empathy, and so on.

Always touch above the waist on the arm. Use a gentle movement: a quick landing, a brief connection, then off again.

Figure 10-9 shows a couple that have just shared a joke. He's used the opportunity to touch her arm to show that not only are they connecting but he also thinks her joke is funny.

Avoid patronising or dominant moves such as putting your arm around someone. Stay above the waist on the arm until you're well acquainted. Touching someone's face is only appropriate when you're very familiar with them and are welcome in their personal/intimate space.

Figure 10-9: Intentional touching.

Preening in Public

Preening in public is exactly how Mother Nature prepared you to attract a mate. The jungle is full of exotic creatures displaying themselves at their best to create the best chance of attracting the fittest mate. The situation's no different for humans; so don't be shy and get ready to shake your tail feathers!

Provocative displays

Unlike the animal kingdom where the males (which are the brightly coloured or striking looking half of the union) are usually putting on the display, the females do most of the displaying in humans. They're giving a clear signal to let men know they're looking. Regardless of gender, the type of display you put on depends on how adventurous you are as a flirt.

The pose in Figure 10-10 is a full-on invitation. A woman directs this look at a particular person, she doesn't use it for generalised attention seeking. This pose is so effective because lifting her arms above her head shows off her vulnerable neck area and exposes the underarm, gives her an instant bust lift, and creates a curve to her spine. The eye contact says she means business and the slightly closed-lip smile shows she's holding something back. He's going to have to come closer if he wants to find out what her secret is.

A man may lead with his crotch thrusted forwards, with his fingers or thumbs pointing at his crotch, and his toes pointing in the direction of a woman to signal sexual interest.

For more gender-specific preening behaviours, see Chapter 12.

Hairy stuff: The role of hair play

Hair play is important. Used by both sexes, twiddling with your hair is a way of showing that you're grooming yourself to be at your very best for the object of your desire. Hair play can involve:

- Smoothing the hair down
- Tucking hair behind the ears to reveal more of the face
- Hair twiddling
- Hair tossing
- A hair show (as shown in Figure 10-10)

Figure 10-10: A provocative display.

Clearly the amount and length of hair you possess limits the range of hair play you can use.

Practise with the types of hair play above to see what works best for you and your hairstyle. Avoid frenetic or wild hair play, however, as you'll just give the impression of being nervous or odd.

Hair play is especially important for women. If a woman finds a man attractive she releases pheromones, a sex hormone. Playing with her hair provocatively releases pheromones from her armpit as she raises her arms, so that by the time he's made his way to her side, he's walking into a great big cloud of the stuff and his olfactory senses are driven wild by the chemical connection.

A good move for a woman wearing her hair pulled back is to unclip it, allowing her hair to tumble to her shoulders. The 'bed head' look is also effective, as it conjures up images of how the hair got to be so tousled.

Chapter 11

Letting Your Body Do the Talking

Making sure that you give off the right signals to the person you're interested in, which I cover in Chapter 10, isn't enough on its own. You then need to build on this and be aware of what signals and clues you're looking for in the other person, and know how the two combine to make a heady flirting cocktail. That's where this chapter comes in.

Being able to spot someone who's fibbing is also useful; relationships need to start from a position of trust. For someone to tell a little white lie about their age, or tell someone that they don't look fat in that dress isn't so much of a problem, but if they have a spouse and half a dozen kids at home, figuring out they're dishonest sooner rather than later is so much better.

Don't forget that the majority of these tips help you gain new friends and win over colleagues, as well as bag dates, so to be popular in and out of work, practise them all! The more you practise, the luckier you get!

Filling Your Space Confidently

Height is one of the most common responses I get when asking women what they look for in a man. However, what actually appeals to them isn't height but stature. A very tall man skulking about with rounded shoulders is very unappealing. A man of more modest height, who carries himself well, with his shoulders back and his chest out, is far more attractive. The difference is stature.

People of either sex who have good stature fill their space well, look more confident, and are more attractive as a result. To be recognised as a flirting prospect you have to be able to stand out from the crowd. To stand out, you need to be spatially dominant, which simply means filling the space around you. Filling your space helps you stand out from other competitors, whether you're flirting or working.

To achieve good posture and spatial dominance:

- ✔ Stand with your feet hip-width apart.

- ✔ Keep your arms away from your body.

- ✔ Keep your head up, your eyes looking forward, and your shoulders back.

If you had to choose a person to flirt with from the people shown in Figure 11-1 on posture alone, you'd probably pick the one on the right because he demonstrates greater balance and presence. The guy on the left is unbalanced, has his head dropped, and, with his arms folded, is taking up the minimum possible amount of space; he's trying to be invisible.

Beware of becoming too spatially dominant by having your legs wide apart and your arms behind your head; this posture can be interpreted as intimidating or arrogant.

Be aware that, while dominating your space is key to getting noticed, getting closer is a key aim if you want your flirtation to progress to a romantic level. To offer a subtle invitation for them to join you, you need to remove the barriers to your space, such as wine glasses, and leave the path clear. Notice how the woman in Figure 11-2 moves from playing coy to leaning in closer, to opening a path towards her with her arm in Figure 11-3.

Figure 11-1: No spatial dominance (left); good spatial dominance (right).

Figure 11-2: Playing coy.

Figure 11-3: Creating an invitation to your space.

For more information on how to invite people into your space, see Chapter 10.

Mirroring Gestures

Mirroring is a way of bonding with another person, creating rapport, and being accepted. This behaviour's a hang over from our prehistoric ancestors, who used it as a way to integrate into larger groups. These days we scan for mirroring behaviour, that is, checking the other person's body language to see if they're moving in the same way or using similar gestures to us, to quickly assess if the other person's feelings toward us are positive or negative.

You're naturally inclined to mirror behaviour because this form of bonding with another person began in the womb when your body functions matched those of your mother.

You may find that consciously mirroring bigger movements helps you to build rapport. But be careful not to copy someone's every move. This behaviour is known as *aping* and when a person spots it, all your rapport building is worthless because it feels manipulative.

Mirroring is your body's non-verbal way of saying, 'Hey, look at me, I'm just like you; we have sooo much in common.' Mirroring isn't just confined to copying the bigger limb movements, postures, and positions such as crossing and uncrossing legs and arms; it also involves smaller, subtler movements such as facial gestures, hand positions, and head nods and tilts.

Mirroring also involves micro gestures, such as:

- ✔ Breathing patterns
- ✔ Blinking patterns
- ✔ Nostril flaring
- ✔ Eyebrow raising/flashing
- ✔ Pupil dilating

These micro gestures cannot easily be consciously imitated, and pupil dilating cannot be deliberately mirrored, so if this level of mirroring is evident, true rapport exists between you.

Positioning the body

Copying is the highest form of flattery, so how better to pay someone a compliment than by adopting their body position.

You can see in Figure 11-4 that almost perfect body mirroring is occurring. Their bodies are leaning at the same angle, they're sitting at the same angle to each other, their legs are angled and pointed opposite to each other, and they're even extending their arms across each other. This pair is enjoying great rapport. If you can effortlessly achieve body mirroring like this, you'll enjoy a great flirtation.

Figure 11-4: Body position mirroring.

Cross your leg and see if they follow. Wait a few minutes, then try something else. If they don't mirror your gesture, try mirroring theirs and then use another limb move.

If they're doing the opposite of mirroring and changing their position so fast you can't possibly keep up and look natural, you're moving too swiftly for them. Back off and build your rapport at a slower pace. They're not ready to make that level of connection yet.

Getting a limb in

As an extension, you can use mirroring as an opportunity to increase body language rapport. Mirroring a limb movement not only gets a limb into the other person's space, bringing you closer, it gives them an opportunity for intentional touching or a bit of accidental brushing against you. This mirroring strategy is perfect if you're not feeling brave enough to be the first one to touch. You can see in Figure 11-5 that where she has crossed her legs to point them towards him, mirroring his leg positioning pointing towards her, that her leg is well into his space, so if he wants to move he's going to have to brush against her. You can also see that she's mirrored his position with subtle changes, so it doesn't come across as aping his exact position.

Mirroring hands placed along the back of a seat you're both sharing, or mirroring a leg crossed across the path of your intended, work equally well in achieving intentional or accidental touching.

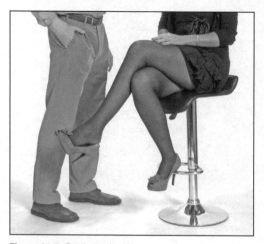

Figure 11-5: Getting a limb in.

Mirroring touch

Mirroring their touching is an excellent way to reassure the other person that their touch has been well received and also to copy their action, so building your rapport and level of attraction for each other.

Use your fingertips and skim, rather than press or grab, the other person.

The safest places to return a touch are:

✔ Back of hand

✔ Forearm

✔ Upper arm

✔ Shoulder

You can mirror and accentuate the touch by placing your hand on them (if they've touched the front of you), as in Figure 11-6.

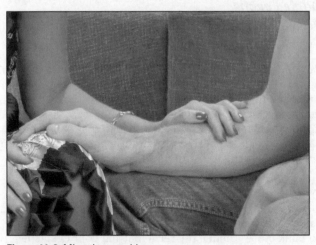

Figure 11-6: Mirroring touching.

Mirroring micro gestures

The information here on micro gestures can help you to see what impact the flirting signals you're giving off are having on the other person.

Blinkin' marvellous

Stewart and Liz were on a course together. They'd met for the first time that day and were getting on famously. Liz really fancied Stewart, but she couldn't tell if he was just being friendly or something more. Over lunch Stewart gave her a blink he hadn't done before. He smiled and raised his shoulders whilst squeezing his eyes shut, as if he was giving her a virtual hug. Liz loved his little blinking gesture and copied it. These little blinks continued, and she noticed that he'd started to copy the little twist to her mouth. She was sure now that this mirroring was more than just coincidence.

Liz and Stewart have been together ever since, and the squeezy blink remains their secret signal to each other if they're in a crowd or if one of them needs a bit of reassurance.

When you're making eye contact during conversation, blinking is hard to miss. To check for rapport, give them a slightly slower blink than usual and see if they respond.

Dilated pupils

People have no control over dilating their pupils, so if you spot this sign in someone, they genuinely fancy you.

Bear in mind that the amount of light in the room has a big impact on the dilation of the pupils, for example if it's very bright, the pupils contract to protect the eye from the harshness, or if it's very dark, the pupils dilate to enable the best vision. Therefore, although dilated pupils are a good sign that someone is attracted to you, you should also check out the lighting in the room to see if that's influencing the situation.

Rapid blinking

Of course, dilated pupils aren't the only way the eyes can reveal interest. If someone looks at you and likes what they see, they tend to blink more – hence the term 'batting your eyelashes'. The brain associates rapid blinking with finding someone sexually attractive, so the more you find yourself blinking at them, the more attracted you can feel towards them.

Just because rapid blinking means they like what they see, don't interpret slow blinking as a lack of interest. If they're completely fascinated or absorbed by you, they may blink very little, as they won't want to miss a thing.

Increase the blink rate of the person you're talking to by blinking more often. If they like you, their blinking synchronises with yours, which in turn makes you feel more attracted to each other as a result of the increased rapport.

Try a discreet wink with a sexy smile. This gesture's great for bonding because it implies the two of you are closer to each other than to the other people around you.

There's more on eye contact in Chapter 10.

Eyebrow raising/flashing

People flash their eyebrows far more than they realise. However, if you consciously try to do it, you'll find yourself pulling a wonderful facial contortion with your brows raising much higher than they would do naturally, and achieving more a look of great surprise.

People raise or flash their eyebrows:

- ✔ **In recognition:** Usually a split second, up–down of the eyebrows.

- ✔ **In surprise:** More exaggerated movements than in recognition. The eyebrows are pulled up the forehead, causing the brow to wrinkle and it can last longer than a raise of the eyebrows in recognition, depending on how surprised they are.

- ✔ **In question:** Think Roger Moore and his amazing single-brow raise, or two if your eyebrows don't work independently. This raise is often accompanied with a forward head tilt and shows that a person isn't sure, is doubtful, or is questioning of you or something you've said.

Breathing

Where you breathe from affects the frequency of your breathing patterns. For example, some people breathe from their stomach or diaphragm, giving them long, deep breaths that can be easier to control; you can spot someone doing this if their stomach goes in and out as they breathe. However, if they breathe from their chest, the chest rises and falls as they do so.

If a person is relaxed, their breathing pattern is slow and deep. If anxious or excited, it's more rapid and comes from higher up in the chest. Feeling passionate can literally make you feel light-headed because the faster breathing brings about too many breaths and creates a mild hyperventilation situation.

Watch for how and from where the other person breathes. Matching or pacing the person's breathing pattern is a powerful way of building rapport. People who breathe at the same rate are usually in synch with each other. For example, when making love, breathing normally is matched breath for breath. People sitting next to each other to watch a film often breathe in synch with each other, especially if the movie is particularly dramatic or eerie.

Nostril flaring

You can clearly see nostril flaring either when someone is afraid (as a primitive way of improving our sense of nearby attackers or of imminent danger) or as a sign of sexual arousal. Nostril flaring is a throw back to the days when we would use our chemical senses to find the best mate. When you see it in someone, they're literally sniffing you out!

Reading Body Language

Body language speaks louder than words; you reveal all your thoughts, moods, and attitudes through it. You can also read the conscious and subconscious thoughts of the person you're flirting with by simply observing what they are or are not doing.

Rule of four

I've heard so many people comment that somebody doesn't like them or is feeling defensive just because they've seen them cross their arms. Interpreting this gesture in these ways is a classic mistake: one movement alone doesn't create a mood or intention. The person could be feeling cold, trying to disguise a spare tyre, or even concealing a stain on their clothes. In the same way that you don't take a word in isolation and determine an exact meaning for it (you don't know whether the word 'tea' refers to a cup of tea or a meal until you see or hear it in a sentence, for example), you can't really know what an isolated gesture truly means. Just as you look for words in a sentence to extrapolate the meaning of other words, gestures come in sentences called *clusters*. A cluster needs at least three gestures, and ideally four, in it before you can accurately interpret its meaning.

Never interpret one body language movement or gesture in isolation, because you're likely to misinterpret what is being conveyed. Instead, stick to the 'Rule of four' when interpreting flirting gestures: aim to spot four body language changes before deciding what you think the movements mean.

Signs revealing how they feel about you

'How can I tell if they like me?' is one of the most commonly asked questions when it comes to the flirting game. The answer is simple – you look for increasingly positive changes in their body language.

As well as telling when someone likes you, being able to spot if your flirtation's going off the boil is also important. Cooling off can happen for many reasons, and thinking back to the time when their body language started to change can give you a good indication as to whether it was something you said or circumstances beyond your control.

Table 11-1 lists signs showing they like you and signs showing they don't. A minimum of three of the positive gestures (those on the 'They Like Me!' list) lets you know they're keen, but a cluster of four is the winning number of changes to be on the sure side. The same practice goes for the 'They Like Me Not' list. Of course, the more you like each other, the more of the positive signs you see.

Table 11-1	Clues to Whether They Like You
They Like Me!	*They Like Me Not*
Increasing eye contact	Declining eye contact
Increasing amount of smiling	Declining or no smiling
Creating closer proximity	Increasing the distance between you
Touching intentionally	Touching isn't reciprocated
Getting a limb in	Retracting their limbs into a smaller space than previously
Mirroring body language	Declining or no mirroring of body language
Mirroring facial language	Declining or no mirroring of facial language
Preening	Declining or no preening
Pointing their feet towards you	Pointing their feet away from you
Playing with objects, such as glasses	Becoming less animated, more still, and unresponsive

Getting colder

Jules and Andrew met by chance in a bar and were getting on famously; Andrew was receiving positive signs that Jules liked him. Suddenly he noticed that she was offering fewer signals and the flirtation seemed to be dwindling. He replayed their conversation in his head to the point at which he first started to notice that her body language was changing; it was when he mentioned that he was visiting his grandfather at the weekend. He couldn't decide if he'd said something to upset her or if she was just going off him. 'You've not been the same since I mentioned my grandfather; is everything okay?' he asked. She said that her grandfather had died recently and that his mention of spending time with his had upset her. Andrew could see she was upset, so he called her a cab and sent her home, taking care to get her number so that he could check she was okay. He called the next day and Jules was delighted to hear from him. She was also really touched that he'd noticed her distress the previous evening. Andrew could've misinterpreted the situation and wrongly assumed that she didn't fancy him; with a bit of detective work, however, he managed to get to the root of the problem and to retrieve the flirtation.

If the flirtation's waning, never assume that you're the problem; cooling off can happen for many reasons.

Avoiding Body Language Mistakes

Doing all the right body language stuff is great, but avoiding or correcting body language that could flatten or kill off your flirtation is equally important.

Lacking eye contact

Making eye contact is one of the most important body language signals. A lack of eye contact can convey:

- ✔ A lack of confidence, if the eyes are cast down
- ✔ Disinterest in the other person, if the eyes are focused on something else (for example, examining the fingernails, lingering reading a text, and so on)
- ✔ Arrogance or disdain, if the eyes are focused upward

You can see in Figure 11-7 that the woman is making conversation. The body language rules of conversation dictate that the listener should make more eye contact than the speaker. The man displays quite the opposite; his eyes raised to the ceiling convey arrogance and disinterest in her. This flirtation is doomed to fail.

Figure 11-7: Lacking eye contact.

If you're not used to making eye contact, practise looking at the bridge of the other person's nose or the top of their head, dropping your eye contact to meet theirs for a time, and taking your gaze back to the top of their head in between. This little routine trains you to get used to looking in the right direction until you're comfortable enough to make proper eye contact; it also creates an impression of supreme confidence!

Floor gazing may be a comfortable habit for you but is extremely unnerving for the other person. Floor gazers generally have rounded shoulders and poor posture. To achieve great deportment and an instantly confident look, hold your head high, roll your shoulders back, and keep your stomach tucked in.

Smile, you're on camera

A group of delegates were being filmed giving a presentation for a body language feedback session I was doing the next day. One delegate in particular stood out; he made no eye contact with his fellow presenters and spent most of the time looking at the floor. He looked as if he lacked confidence and didn't seem to gel well with his colleagues. Then I noticed his hand creeping up and down his arm; it was an odd movement and looked like he wanted to scratch his nose. Eventually he bowed his head even lower and had a good rummage up his nose. It wasn't the most pro-fessional of things to do in a presentation, never mind one that was being filmed! The next day we replayed the tapes and he was very embarrassed. I asked why he picked his nose during the presentation and he said he didn't think anyone would see; he'd spent his life looking at the floor and assumed everyone else did too. It turned out that he was much more confident than he appeared and was actually regarded as a valued member of the team. Simply correcting where he trained his eyes made him appear more confident and engaging.

Unless you've got your eye on the game you won't know what's going on around you. Keep your gaze focusing upward to remain in the action and avoid unneces-sary social gaffes.

Wrapping like a python

People who python wrap try to take up as little space as possible. They touch themselves all over for reassurance and to be as unnoticeable as possible. Unfortunately they then stand out for all the wrong reasons.

You can see in Figure 11-8 that the man's posture is very negative, which significantly affects his attitude and makes him more defensive and resistant to approaches. By having such a closed posture, he's effectively making a barrier between himself and the rest of the world.

To avoid the python wrap, roll your shoulders back and stand with your feet hip-width apart. Try holding something in your hands, such as a pen, glass, or paper, to stop them crossing over your chest.

Figure 11-8: The python wrap.

Leaning away

People who lean away from another person aren't closing the proximity gap, they're making it bigger. Doing so makes building rapport harder and flirting slower. Figure 11-9 shows the man angled away because the woman is leaning away from him.

If you do fancy the other person – and they like the look of you – but are leaning away because you're shy, you could inadvertently mirror each other's negative body language and make the flirtation spiral backwards.

Always lean in slightly and make good eye contact when you talk to avoid sending the wrong signals.

Figure 11-9: Leaning away.

Letting it all hang out

The body language of Saddam Hussein when he was being interviewed just before Iraq was invaded spoke volumes about him and his attitude toward the threats from the West. He sat slumped back in his big chair, gesticulating casually as he talked, with his legs spread wide apart. I can't care less, his posture said, I'm so non-plussed I can't even bother to look aggressive.

Whether standing or sitting, this kind of bad body language screams disinterested slob. If you can't even make the effort to stand or sit properly, how on earth are you going to carry off a flirtation? Any flirt worth their salt is going to pass you by for a better prospect.

The guy in Figure 11-10 doesn't care and can't make the effort to stand up straight. He'll struggle making an effort on any other front, too, including flirting. Even the line of his clothes is ruined where he's bunched his hands up in his pockets.

Aim to stand or sit two inches higher than your actual height. Ask close friends and colleagues to tell you when you're slumping to get used to holding a good posture at all times.

Figure 11-10: Letting it all hang out.

Fiddling

Playing, twirling, and fiddling can be indicative of a number of emotions. For example, children that bite their nails and frequently pull or play with their hair may be nervous or have low self-esteem. Hair twirling may be a comforting action for a child who is tense and anxious, and may become habitual later in life in stressful situations.

Fiddling can make you look nervous or untrustworthy, neither of which are good looks when flirting. Excessive fiddling can also indicate anxiety or nerves and can be seen demonstrated in a number of areas:

✔ Clothes, particularly buttons, zips, cuffs, and collars

✔ Necklaces

✔ Pens

✔ Glasses

✔ Cigarettes

✔ Phones

 Ask a friend whether you have a tendency to fiddle and what you play around with most. Break your fiddling habit by using diversionary tactics, for example if you click pens, carry a pencil instead; wear a brooch rather than a necklace if you can't stop pulling at it.

 Get a friend to give you a signal that you're fiddling. When you see the signal, put your hands on your lap (if you're sitting) and take three long breaths. Doing so calms you down, re-sets your breathing, and controls your nerves and anxiety.

 Fiddling can sometimes signify different things in different situations. Take fiddling with your hair. Hair twirling can demonstrate interest and desire (as mentioned in Chapter 10), but in other situations it can signify anxiety, uncertainty, or shyness. Be careful that a provocative twiddle of your hair (or playing with the stem of your glass) doesn't become frenetic when you're nervous or excited and spoil the illusion of your super cool flirtation.

Using Your Hands

More connections exist between the hands and the brain than any other part of the body. As well as being a vital tool, throughout history hand gestures, particularly that of the open palm, have demonstrated honesty and trustworthiness, as well as allegiance and submission. Even today, many oaths are taken with the flat palm of the hand over the heart. You also have to show the palm of your hand when being sworn in in court. What better tool for showing the person you're flirting with that you're honest and trustworthy – vital keystones when building the foundations of relationships both at work and play.

Thumbs up

Assertive or dominant people usually have their thumbs on display. In palmistry, the thumbs are considered to denote strength of character and superiority. Men often fold their arms across their chest with their fingers under their arms and both thumbs visible and pointing upwards, signalling confidence. Confident women tend to leave their thumbs out when they put their hands in their pockets and angle their arms away from the side of the body, creating the impression of stature and of filling more space – as you can see in Figure 11-11.

Steepling, where the hands are placed together with just the finger and thumb tips touching, is also seen as a sign of self-confidence.

Figure 11-11: Confident women with thumbs out.

Handy info

The hands reveal a lot about your emotional state and are very easy to see because they're always in front of you. Keep your eye out for the following common gestures – demonstrated by other people and also yourself.

Palms, hidden or exposed

When being truthful, you're likely to expose your palms; this completely natural gesture gives the other person an intuitive feeling that you're being honest. The palms are the vocal cords of body language. Hiding them is the equivalent of keeping your mouth shut.

Try not to turn your hands so their backs face the person you're flirting with; open palm and wrist displays are not only more aesthetically appealing, they also signal openness and honesty.

Auto-erotic gestures

Using auto-erotic gestures, such as putting your finger in your mouth, can be very sexy in a flirtation (see Figure 11-12). However, putting your fingers in your mouth and biting your nails isn't an attractive look, and the more nervous or anxious you become, the more of your hand you'll try to get in there. (Psychologists say this behaviour's an attempt to revert to the security of breastfeeding.)

Figure 11-12: Auto-erotic gestures.

Hand clenches

Hand clenching refers to the interlocking of your fingers in front of your body. This gesture can signify restraint, but if your hands start to clench so tightly that your fingers whiten, you're demonstrating nerves or anxiety. The higher the hands are clenched in front of you or the other person, the higher the degree of anxiety.

If the person you're flirting with is clenching their hands, get them to relax by giving them something to hold, such as a drink.

Interested evaluations

Often, when someone's evaluating what you've said, they rest a closed hand on their chin or cheek, sometimes with the index finger pointing skyward. This gesture's a positive sign because they're really considering what you're talking about.

Watch for the hand slipping to under the chin and becoming a support for the head – this person has moved from evaluation to boredom, as shown in Figure 11-13.

Figure 11-13: A negative evaluation gesture.

Chin stroking

Chin stroking, as shown in Figure 11-14, shows that the person is thinking about your conversation and is reaching a mental decision. In flirting terms, that decision may relate to whether they like you or believe what you've said.

Chin stroking can also make someone look more contemplative and engrossed in what the other person is saying.

Figure 11-14: Chin stroking.

Making barriers

The hands can be effective tools to not only welcome somebody into your space, but also to keep them at a distance. For example, resting your clenched hand on the table in front of you not only demonstrates your reserve but also that you're defending this little bit of territory. This gesture's not very welcoming to the other person and is a clear signal that you want them to keep their distance.

You can avoid making barriers by keeping your palms on display at all times. See the earlier section 'Palms, hidden or exposed' for more info.

If you're faced with a hand barrier, use a diversionary tactic such as giving them something to hold, or moving to another location to get them to open up.

Spotting a Liar

Life would be easier if 'Liar, liar, pants on fire' were true and you could spot a fibber straight off. In fact, all the squirming and wriggling that liars do does create the impression of their pants being on fire. Thanks to all the little clues that liars give us, though, you don't have to wait for them to spontaneously combust to see when they're telling porkies.

Discovering that your flirtation is based on lies can be very demoralising and upsetting, depending on how big the lies are and how many you hear from someone. Being aware of lying behaviour and the clues that give it away enables you to walk away from a liar before you get unwittingly dragged into their web of deceit.

Going through life without telling a single lie is almost impossible. If you were completely honest all of the time, you'd probably be quite friendless before long. White lies are the little untruths that grease our social interaction with others and help us maintain friendly relationships; sometimes telling a white lie rather than the cold hard truth is kinder. However, malicious liars – those who deliberately attempt to deceive you for their personal benefit need to be avoided.

Here are a couple of interesting facts about liars and lying:

- ✔ Research shows that social liars are more popular than people who dogmatically tell the truth, even though you know that a social liar is lying to you.

  Don't cast off the flirtatious advances of someone who's guilty of a bit of insincere flattery rather than being an outright liar.

- ✔ Women are better at spotting a lie. Many people think that this is because women have evolved as the carers and men as the hunter–gatherers, and so have more honed non-verbal reading skills from caring for infants who can't yet speak. This means that women have a more natural bent for spotting incongruencies between what's being said and how the person is behaving, which gives the lie away.

- ✔ People who routinely or compulsively lie, or who tell spectacularly elaborate lies are best avoided because this characteristic indicates that they find the truth difficult to handle, or that they can't deal with conflict.

Recognising a bad-un through body language

Reliable clues as to whether someone is lying can be spotted in their body language rather than their words. The liar gets a chance to rehearse their words and so can control that aspect of the lie. They have much less control over their gestures, however, as these happen automatically and are mostly subconscious.

They're definitely lying

When playing a game in which a group was asked to identify a liar from a line up of people telling a story, they were unanimous in their choice. 'It's definitely him. He stumbled and fidgeted his way through the story and looked so uncomfortable, he had to be lying,' agreed the group – with one exception, who was adamant it wasn't him. When he was asked to justify his decision, he replied, 'I'm his boss and he always acts like that.'

If someone is naturally fidgety and jumpy, they probably just experience high levels of nervous energy or anxiety. Look for behaviour that's out of context before you condemn an innocent person for lying.

When lying, the body sends out nervous energy, a subconscious clue, which manifests itself as a gesture that isn't congruent with what is being said. Accomplished liars often prefer to lie by omission and have managed to hone the lying process and refine their gestures to the point where they're very difficult to spot.

You need to be aware of a number of common gestures indicating deception. Thinking of the three wise monkeys who hear no evil, see no evil, and speak no evil helps you remember them.

As with interpreting all gestures, they need to be read in context to be meaningful. It helps to know the person, because you can then measure their expressions and gestures against their normal behaviour. Look for at least three changes before you jump to con-clusions. One nose touch could indicate a cold rather than a liar. Look at their gestures in the context of the conversations you've been having with them; are they markedly different? Has the pat-tern and pace of their conversation or their tone of voice changed in relation to the gestures you're observing? If not, they're proba-bly just scratching an itch.

Hear no evil

Grabbing or pulling at the ear when someone is responding to something you've said can indicate that, although they're agreeing with you, they're actually covering up their true feelings. This gesture reveals anxiety in the other person.

See no evil

Rubbing of the eyes is the brain's attempt to ignore the deceit being acted out upon another person. Research shows that men are more likely to employ this gesture than women, who prefer a gentle rub of the eye or to look away altogether. Men rub the eye vigorously, but may also look away if telling a whopper.

The alternative to averting the eyes when lying is looking the person you're deceiving directly in the eye. Here, you'll notice them making more eye contact than usual; the eyes will be less friendly and they may dart before they speak. Liars have no control over this tiny movement.

Speak no evil

In this gesture, the hand covers the mouth as if the brain has subconsciously told it to prevent the fib from passing the lips. Whether the person uses a few fingers or the whole hand, the meaning's the same: they're attempting to cover a lie.

If they cover their mouths whilst you're speaking, they could be indicating that they think you're hiding something.

Rubbing and scratching

Pulling at the collar, rubbing the neck, and scratching or touching the nose are other indicators that a fib may be on the way. Lying increases the blood pressure, causing tissues to dilate and hence the nose to itch and the collar to feel tight.

Finding telltale clues in conversation

Whilst a liar may rehearse their words in order to deceive you, little clues in their language can give their game away.

When trying to deceive you, their pattern of speech and pitch are likely to change. They probably speak in a higher pitch than usual. They may also end their sentences with a rising inflection, as if questioning what they're saying themselves.

When recounting their fib, liars are prone to make errors in their speech and may hesitate more. They'll also babble to fill in the gaps in conversation.

The words a liar may use can also lead you to conclude they're not being completely honest with you. If a person talks about absolutes but uses words such as 'probably', 'likely', or 'sort of', they may be lying to you. For example, if someone said they stood you up because they 'sort of' got held up so they didn't 'quite' make it, and they 'think' they left their phone at home so couldn't 'really' call you, their words may not be completely truthful. If that person had been telling the truth, their words would have been different: 'I'd been held up and was therefore unable to make it; plus I'd left my phone at home and I'm sorry I didn't call you'.

What's not your birthday present?

My daughter, Lucy, was a spectacular fibber as a child. She was so gorgeous looking that everybody let her get away with it. Thankfully, I was just as cunning at finding her out. One year my father bought her birthday present and hid it in a spare room in our house. I told Lucy not to go into the room. Being Lucy, however, she couldn't resist, and she took her brother along as accomplice to the naughty deed. Calum couldn't lie for toffee. His face said, 'Please catch me out, I can't live with the guilt' and I immediately knew where they'd been. On being interrogated, Calum stayed quiet and Lucy, very convincingly, did all the talking, denying any such act and claiming she didn't know what grandpa had bought her for her birthday. Eventually, to prove she hadn't been into the room, I asked her to guess what her grandfather hadn't bought her for her birthday. 'Well, I don't think he's bought me an air hockey game,' she announced in a high pitched voice, raised in a question – and actually he had.

Getting your story straight before telling a lie is easy, but if any interrogation, albeit mild, follows, the lies have a habit of showing themselves.

Research shows that women are better liars than men and prefer more complicated stories. Men prefer to stick to simple lies. Interestingly, attractive people are more believable than unattractive people.

Disentangling from a liar

Some people prefer to stay flirting with a liar because:

- ✔ Believing that the person is being truthful is easier than facing the fact that you're being deceived.

- ✔ They don't like conflict and prefer to ignore the situation, hoping that the liar modifies their own behaviour of their own accord.

Either of these scenarios can be a recipe for disaster because a liar believing they've convincingly deceived the other person can lead to bigger and more elaborate lies.

If you think a person has lied to you over just one thing and they've not yet spun a web of lies, then they may have a reason for the deceit. If you can get to the bottom of it, you may have a basis for continuing the flirtation; if not, then it's time to walk away.

If you think that someone has told you several lies, you can either confront the liar and ask them to validate what they've said or ask them lots of open questions until they trip themselves up. All this actually achieves, though, is proving that the person is a liar. If someone can't be honest with you this early on in a relationship, your best option is simply to walk away.

Letting Them Down Gently

Sometimes, for whatever reason, you decide that the other person isn't for you. Regardless of whether you've given them no encouragement, they're just a friend, or you're in the middle of a flirtation, stopping their advances can be very difficult and awkward. Thankfully, you can let that person down very gently, without the need for words, by sending them appropriate messages through your body language.

Don't wait until you're at breaking point to deflect unwanted attention; tackling it sooner rather than later is the most effective option.

Subtly showing you're not interested

By using a cluster of gestures you can let the other person know you're not interested without saying a word. The hand gestures mentioned in the preceding section are a great way to start getting your message across.

A chin stroke followed by a lean back in your seat, or a head resting on your hand, accompanied by less smiling, less eye contact, and shorter responses, lets them clearly see that you're not interested. Maintaining rapport without the essential body language is impossible and they'll eventually give up. If they don't get the message, check out Chapter 18 on how to off-load overly persistent admirers.

Using barriers to slow them down

If you're not sure if you like someone and you want them to tone their approach down, use barriers to stall them. Consider these tactics:

> ✔ Use the hand clench extended on the table, as described in the earlier section 'Making barriers', to create more space and defend yourself.

✔ Use props (anything from a menu to your handbag) to create a physical barrier between you. When they detect that things are cooling off, they'll back off. Figure 11-15 shows a woman using her handbag as a barrier. Also notice the other signs that she's no longer interested: she's angled away and her knees and feet are pointing in the direction in which she'd like to go. Within a couple of sentences this chap will be getting the message loud and clear that she's not interested.

If you want to get away from someone, point your feet in the direction in which you'd like to travel. Doing so provides a message to yourself that you intend to leave and one to them that you're going.

Figure 11-15: Using barriers.

Chapter 12

Reading Secret Flirting Signals

As well as the general flirting signals and body language (explained in the preceding two chapters), more gender-specific tips exist to tell if someone wants to be more than just friends. See if you can spot the extra tell-tale signals that give their game away – then act on them!

Both men and women make use of their body movements and facial gestures to flirt. They preen; they smile; they make use of their eyes to convey interest. However, subtle differences between the sexes' flirting signals exist, and knowing what to expect can help you to avoid any misunderstandings and lead to a fruitful flirtation.

Reading and Reacting to Female Flirting Signals

Women have some extra flirting clues that are peculiar to the fairer sex. Look out for these in addition to the clues you've gleaned already.

Spotting facial clues

You may know the old saying 'a face can tell a thousand stories'. In the midst of a flirtation you can certainly tell a lot from a woman's facial expression, particularly by knowing how to read her eyes and mouth movements.

Eyes

Intense feelings cause the tear glands to secrete fluid, but they won't overflow and reduce her to tears unless she's feeling pain or strong emotion. This effect can't be faked and the excess moisture causes the light to reflect off the eye, giving a twinkling effect. As long as you've not just trodden on her toe, if her eyes are sparkling you can view it as a twinkle of excitement.

Mouth

If you excite her, her blood pressure will race and her lips may swell as they fill with blood. Women are spending a small fortune on having their lips filled for good reason: they want to create the impression of being ripe and desirable.

The wetting of the lips, either with saliva or gloss, also creates the impression of sexual invitation. Slightly parted lips offer a signal that she's open to the idea of you. Women also often bite their bottom lip when they find a man attractive.

Understanding proximity clues

The widening or closing of a gap between you and another person can say a lot more than words about the other person's attitude towards you. In the world of flirting the mantra has to be 'the closer the better', and here I look at the unique methods that women employ to make that happen. (You can read more about proximity in Chapter 10.)

Moving closer to you

If a woman brushes behind you in a bar and gently moves you to the side and if she gives you a broad smile when you turn round to let her pass, she's more interested in chatting to you than getting round you. The intentional touch here is no accident; it's guaranteed to get your attention and is a polite way of excusing herself for invading your space. Plus, she's created a perfect invitation for you to talk if you're then stood next to each other at the bar, because you've already spoken and not chatting would be almost rude.

Women move invitingly closer when they're interested in gaining your full attention. Moving her head closer to yours not only blocks everyone else from your radar, it unconsciously prepares the ground for the first kiss. If her head is so close that your eyes are in line with each other but you're still in focus, for example she's not just bending closer so she can hear you speak in a noisy room, then take the initiative and kiss her.

Lowering her voice and almost whispering whilst leaning her head forward is an invitation for you to join her space and get a little more intimate. Lower your voice too and gently move her hair out of the way so that you can talk gently in her ear. Watch the goose bumps rise!

Never approach a woman from behind because it's a threatening approach. Also, it doesn't give you the opportunity to pave the way with your non-verbal flirting gestures. Always approach in her line of vision.

Placing objects in your way

When a woman finds you attractive she's likely to invade your space with objects. You find that her glass works from her side of the table or bar to yours. If she's confident that you like her, she leaves her glass there, with her hand close by in the hope that you touch it.

A woman's handbag is a very personal object; it can contain a lot of her life. If a strange woman puts her handbag next to you, chances are she's interested in you. Asking you to pass her bag to her or to retrieve something from it is an invitation into her inner sanctum. If she keeps her handbag close to her and away from you, however, she's keeping her emotional distance.

Always compliment a woman on her great choice of handbag. Women spend a lot of time and money on bags, so they'll appreciate your noticing. Commenting shows insight on your part and is an obvious initiation to flirt because men are reputed to not commonly notice these things.

If a woman pushes her glass into your space and leaves her hand there, take the initiative and give her hand a gentle touch next time she says something funny or entertaining.

Recognising tactile clues

When they find a man seriously attractive, women use a whole range of auto-erotic touches. You may notice that she starts to touch herself in one or more of the following ways:

- **Massaging her neck:** No, she doesn't need an osteopath, this move gives her an instant breast lift and shows off her armpit, the source of all those lovely pheromones.
- **Preening:** All that fluffing of hair, licking of lips, and arranging of cleavage is to make her appear at her very best for you.
- **Smoothing her hands over her neck and arms:** This marvellous tease aims to make you jealous that it's not your hands sliding over her.

✔ **Using her fingers:** If she's using her fingers to gently brush against her lips or cleavage or playing with a glass or straw, her fingers are acting out what she'd like to be happening. In Figure 12-1, the woman's alternating between running her finger around the rim of her glass and playing with the stem, whilst maintaining eye contact – a clear signal that she's into you.

✔ **The leg twine:** If she's crossing and uncrossing her legs in front of you and gently stroking her thighs, she's indicating a desire to be touched.

When you notice these clues, you can stop doubting and ramp up your flirting technique.

Figure 12-1: Finger play.

Using mirroring clues

Sexually confident women mirror the cowboy stance seen in men (see Figure 12-2): legs apart, weight on one foot, hips tilted, and hands on hips. If you smile at her and she smiles back broadly whilst maintaining eye contact, as in Figure 12-2, consider it a direct invitation for you to go over and talk to her.

A woman who adopts this stance is interested in only the most confident of flirts. If you want to flirt with her, you need to ooze assurance; she'll take no prisoners and has no time for fragile egos.

You can read more about how both sexes employ mirroring tactics in a flirtation in Chapter 11.

Figure 12-2: A sexually confident woman.

Noticing dress and make-up clues

Don't make the mistake of assuming that if a woman's wearing a revealing outfit she's doing so for your benefit. She's wearing it because she feels great in it and the outfit makes her stand out from the crowd. Only when you spot her adjusting her clothes can you assume that you're the one that she wants to see more of her. If, when you return from the bar, she suddenly has an extra button undone on her top or her skirt seems shorter than before, she's made a quick adjustment for your benefit when you weren't looking.

Wearers of red lipstick are adventurous women, not only because red's a difficult colour to pull off (it's such a strong colour with sexy undertones) but also because it screams 'look at me'. Research shows that bright red lipstick is men's favourite. This colour mimics that of the sex organs at the point of climax.

If you're going to wear red lipstick, be aware that it can make your teeth appear yellow unless they're very bright, so always pick the shade of red that suits you best.

If she's wearing glasses and then takes them off and sucks one arm of them seductively whilst making eye contact, she's playing with you and providing a flirtatious feast for your eyes – see Figure 12-3. If, however, she's not smiling or is chewing the arm like an anxious hamster, she's worried, not flirting.

Figure 12-3: Provocative display using glasses.

Reading Male Flirting Signals

Research shows us that women have a range of 52 flirting signals to let men know they're interested; men have approximately 10. Thankfully women are quite adept at spotting and deciphering these clues!

Spotting preening clues

To see if a man's interest in you is more than just passing, look for the following preening clues when you're around a man:

- **Hair:** A guy either smooths or messes up his hair, depending on his hairstyle, to show you that he's trying to display himself at his very best.

- **Smoothing:** When he flattens his tie down or smoothes a lapel, he's using the equivalent move of the female licking of lips. He's trying to appear as groomed and appealing as possible.

- **Touching himself:** If you notice him stroking his cheek with the back of his fingers, or rubbing his chin more often while he's looking at you, he's demonstrating a combination of nervous excitement and preening.

- **Playing with buttons:** If he's fiddling with his buttons he's using a *displacement activity* – where a person uses an action either to comfort themselves or while they're deciding what to do next – because you've made him a bit nervous and he's responding to an unconscious desire to remove his clothes. If he then unbuttons his jacket and props it open with his hands on his hips, then removes it completely, he's subconsciously acting out the next stage of the flirtation.

Seeing where his digits point

A man putting his thumbs in his belt or his hands in his pockets with his digits pointing to his crotch is one of the most obvious sexual displays he can put on for a woman in a public place. These gestures are a little subtler than the codpieces men used to advertise their manhood and status back in the 15th century – tight leather trousers or jeans worn with a lighter colour at the crotch are a modern day comparison – but are still definite signals that he wants you to check him out. If he spends the night with his hands on his hips and his fingers splayed out towards his crotch he's subconsciously willing you to look and touch.

Women routinely complain in my seminars about men 'rummaging' – feeling the need to adjust their crotch, either from inside the trouser pocket or by manhandling it from the outside. Almost as shocking as the initial rummage is when a man then offers you the same hand to shake or passes you a drink with it. However, for the man, this gesture is a sign of masculine assertion and to let you know he's got a package so impressive it needs constant re-adjustment.

Checking his spatial dominance

A man's *spatial dominance* – in other words, how he fills the space around his body – gives you a good indication of his opinion of himself and his level of confidence. How he fills this space when he's around you gives a clue about how he's feeling towards you:

- ✔ **Standing to attention:** He flexes his muscles to show you his physique in the best possible light. If he's standing directly in front of you when he does it, the display's for your eyes only.

- ✔ **Hip-holding stance:** If he's standing with his legs apart and his hands on his hips, he's confident of his body and wants you to notice it.

- ✔ **Guiding hand:** When you're moving through a crowd he'll guide you with his hand on the small of your back or elbow. He's demonstrating to the competition that you're being taken care of and also making sure you don't get lost in the crowd.

> ✔ **Perching:** If he perches on the edge of his seat to get closer to you, particularly if he's crossing his leg and the top leg is pointing in your direction, he's signaling that he fancies you.

If you're receiving these signals, make sure things don't go off track. Reassure him and ramp up your flirting game with plenty of mirroring, and use the female flirting signals described earlier in this chapter.

Flirtatious signals don't necessarily come one at a time. Be on the lookout for clusters of signals (refer to Chapter 11). In Figure 12-4, for example, the guy is not only giving the woman a sitting crotch display with his hand pointing towards his crown jewels, he's smoothing his hair, pointing his feet at her, and engaging her in eye contact. A neon sign couldn't make it clearer that he fancies her.

Figure 12-4: Preening crotch display.

Listening for the changes

Changes in his voice offer a big clue as to how far he's into your flirtation. Initially he'll use lots of bass to show you how big and manly he is. A low voice like Barry White's is hot and sexy, while a high tenor conveys youthful exuberance. As the flirtation wears on his hormones start racing and his breath gets shorter; as you move your heads closer together his voice gets quieter. You've now got him in the palm of your hand.

If you move your head closer towards him, maybe with an accidental brush of your cheek against his, you're offering a clear indication that you want to be more intimate and for him to start whispering directly into your ear

Part IV
Taking the Next Step

"Flirting sort of runs in my family, actually."

In this part . . .

In this part I look at moving your flirtation on, knowing when to leave them wanting more, spotting a liar before you get your fingers burned, and overcoming the fear of rejection to flirt more successfully.

Chapter 13

Making the Next Move

In This Chapter

▶ Working out what your next move should be

▶ Making that next move

▶ Considering seduction strategies

A friendly flirt sits well within most people's comfort zone, but the stumbling block for many is knowing when to turn up the temperature into a full-on flirt and how to get the end result you want, from a telephone number, to a kiss, to an invitation for coffee!

This chapter covers all the tips you need to develop a friendly flirtation into something more romantic.

Making the Next Move: The Logistics

You've been flirting for a while and everything's lovely, but when should you make the next move? Before you actually make the next move, you need to consider two things: whether you actually want to make the next move, and if you do, the venue.

Keen – or not?

If you're over your initial curiosity and you've decided that they're really not for you and you don't want to take things any further, don't string them along under the misapprehension that you're being kind to their feelings. Doing so only causes you more of a problem later when you can't shake them off because you left them with the impression that you wanted to see them again. Most people will think a lot more of you for being straight with them in the first place. Check out Chapter 18 for ways to ditch someone nicely.

Too shy for sure

Adam and Nancy worked for the same company, which employed over 1,000 people. They'd spotted each other going in and out of the building but had exchanged nothing more than glances. At a small function to celebrate the completion of a large project, the two literally bumped into each other. Adam apologised and went to get Nancy a drink. Now the ice was broken the two chatted animatedly together. When the event started to wind up, Adam and Nancy mirrored each other's body language as they shuffled from foot to foot wondering who was going to make the first move. Ultimately, an awkward silence ensued before they said goodbye and headed back to their respective offices. Adam kicked himself for not asking for her number and decided to track her down; hopefully not many Nancys worked in the building and he should be able to recognise her voice. Just as he was leaving the office, however, he received an email from Nancy asking him to join her for coffee, so all ended well.

Don't be afraid to take the initiative or you may not get the opportunity to ask again.

However, if you really like a person and you can see that the feeling is mutual, by them mirroring your words, gestures, and proximity and giving off preening signals, you're ready to make the next move. Whether you've been flirting with a new friend or a date, letting them slip away for the want of taking the initiative is a waste of all your hard work.

If you're wondering about who should make the next move, let's not be old-fashioned about it. Don't leave the guys to do all the running; being chased is flattering for men and women.

Where to make the next move

Deciding where to make the next move can sometimes be tricky. You want the setting to be right and to have a little flirting zone of your own to work within without any distracting interruptions. You may be tempted to wait to get them on their own, but this opportunity may pass you by if they wander off with friends.

In groups

You don't need to announce your desire to take things further in front of a group of people, you can create your own space within the group. Follow these steps:

1. **Turn to face the person.**

   Not only does this move block their view of other people it also makes it very difficult for anyone to interrupt.

2. **If the room is loud, touch them on the upper arm as you lean in to ask the question.**

3. **Pop your question, whether you're asking for a number, date, or invitation back for coffee.**

After you've popped your question, don't stand facing them for too long unless you're both comfortable with the position (that is, you're in a full-on flirt). Otherwise, this stance can be intimidating. Find out more in the later section 'Going for the kiss'.

Asking them if you can have a quiet word can sometimes kill the moment, unless you've a strong indication that the feeling is mutual (for example, they're mirroring your body and facial language, moving closer in proximity to you, and exhibiting preening clues) in which case they'll welcome the opportunity to get a quiet conversation going. However, if you're in any doubt that things are more one-sided, wait until they leave for a comfort break and use the opportunity to have a quiet word on the way to or from the loo.

In the office

Making a move in the office is potentially problematic, particularly if the other person feels compromised or if they could interpret your advance as sexual harassment. If you're going to make your next move with someone in the office, you need to be aware of certain things:

- ✔ If you're not already speaking to the person, never approach them from behind because they won't be at their most receptive when surprised. In a survey of office behaviour, I found that being approached from behind, particularly if the person isn't aware you're behind them, ranked as one of the most irritating behaviours. So avoid doing it.

- ✔ Respect their right to keep their private life private and don't broadcast your move to the rest of the office and their colleagues by telling everyone that you're going to ask them or by asking in front of their colleagues.

- ✔ Be aware of your status in the company compared to theirs and don't make your move in a manner that could be construed as patronising or intimidating (for example sitting on their desk in front of them, leaning over their shoulder from behind and whispering in their ear, or cornering them in the lift).

Office gaffe

Tim had been attracted to Jill, a personal assistant, for ages. He decided he was going to make the bold step of asking her out. Her desk faced the wall, so he walked up behind her, leant over her shoulder, and asked her in a whisper if he could have a word. Tim nonchalantly sat on her desk to face her, before asking in a very audible voice if she was available at the weekend. Jill flushed; she was attracted to Tim, but he'd taken her by surprise. Tim was a manager and he'd asked her in front of her colleagues. She could feel the office go quiet as they all listened in to their conversation, waiting to see if she'd say yes. Jill was in a difficult position; if she said no she'd embarrass him and he wouldn't ask her again, but if she said yes she might appear a pushover in front of her colleagues. Jill went very red, which didn't help the situation. Jill responded that she'd have to check her diary and she'd email him later. Tim had made several errors in judgement in his choice of where to make his move, but Jill rescued the situation nicely and got to make her response without the rest of the office being party to it.

To achieve the result you want, think about the points above before deciding on the best place to make your next move.

✔ Pick neutral zones like the cafeteria, kitchen, or anywhere outside the office setting.

The place that is least conducive towards making your next move is the lift. People find it difficult to talk and deliberately avoid making eye contact in lifts because the situation forces you to let people into your personal space who wouldn't normally be allowed. If you're too close when you make your move, it could be enough to put them off.

Read more about starting an office romance in Chapter 14.

When to make the next move

Pick the right moment to make the next move. Don't wait for it to appear. The clue that tells you that one time may be better than another is when you feel an increase in their body language towards you. For example, they're smiling more at you, have increased their eye contact, are mirroring your body language, their proximity is closer, they're preening themselves or intentionally touching themselves or you, and they're giving you their full attention.

At certain times, making a move isn't advisable:

✔ When you or the other person is drunk or under the influence of drugs, because you may say or do something you later regret.

One-shot wonder

Michelle and Sarah met on a weekend residential course. They got on like a house on fire during the day and on the Saturday night they sat up until the early hours as Michelle regaled Sarah with funny story after funny story. Sarah thought she'd met her new best friend; she'd had the funniest life and they'd bonded so strongly. She invited Michelle to stay the following weekend. They sat up to the early hours again whilst Michelle repeated the stories she'd told the previous weekend. Sarah then realised that Michelle had related all her best anecdotes and had nothing left to tell. Her life had sounded amazing, because she'd basically described everything that had ever happened to her in the space of one evening; unfortunately, she was incapable of making any further conversation.

Michelle had tried so hard to win Sarah's friendship that she'd given too much away, too soon. She was devastated that she'd lost somebody else who could have been her friend. Michelle bought a book on how to build rapport with other people and be charismatic. She started to pace herself and to leave people wanting more. Hinting at having untold stories to reveal did wonders for both maintaining new friendships and her love life.

Always leave them wanting more to maximise the success of your flirtations.

✔ In an atmosphere where seeing or hearing the other person's reaction is difficult, such as a night club.

✔ When the other person has just had some devastating news and is using you as a shoulder to cry on. Don't confuse sharing a highly emotional moment as being anything more than solace; misreading the situation like this may lead to rejection if you make a pass.

✔ When you or the other person is tired or ill, because they may give a negative response that you could misinterpret as rejection, when actually they're just not up to accepting an advance.

✔ When the other person is in a rush, because they may not give your advance the consideration it deserves.

Leave them wanting more

'Always leave them wanting more' is one of the fundamentals of flirting – it applies whether you're making a new friend or a new lover. Leaving them wanting more builds anticipation and makes the next meeting even better. There's really only one effective way of doing this and it's to end your date on a high rather than hanging on in there until the conversation runs dry.

If no natural break occurs in the conversation, make an excuse to leave. Doing so leaves them hungry to see more of you and moves you swiftly into the 'assessing what your next move should be' phase, as covered in the next section.

Assessing What the Next Move Should Be

No hard and fast rules exist about what the next move should be; just make sure you're comfortable with it and that events occur at your own pace. Don't be pushed into doing anything you're not ready for. Some people are happy to hit the hay on the first date; others are quite satisfied with swapping numbers. Personal preference is what matters; you're no more or less of a flirt judged by how far you do or don't get.

Alcohol suppresses inhibition and we tend to do silly things and things we may regret when we've had a drink. If you don't want to do anything on your date that you may regret, lay off the booze.

Asking for their number

Whether you're enjoying a full-on flirtation with someone or just making a new friend, getting their number is a must if you're unlikely to bump into them again. You've already done the hard part; asking for their number is a piece of cake in comparison.

Don't hope that they're going to ask for your number and wait for them to do so; they could be waiting for you to ask.

When you sense that the conversation is coming to a close or you're ready to leave them wanting more:

1. **Thank them for their company and say how much you've enjoyed being with them.**

2. **Tell them that seeing them again – for lunch, coffee, drinks, dinner, or whatever you feel is appropriate – would be good.**

3. **If they agree, organise a time and place to meet up there and then, or ask for their number and tell them roughly when you'll call, or give them your number and tell them the best time to call you.**

Don't forget to either have a pen handy or punch the number straight into your mobile phone.

Going for the kiss

Sometimes you just know when the time is right for a kiss, but if you're lacking in flirting confidence you may not be able to go for it. Recognising whether they're ready to kiss you can help. Following are some signals that the person you're flirting with would be happy with a kiss:

- ✔ Your heads have become noticeably closer together.

- ✔ They're looking at your mouth more.

- ✔ They're touching their mouth and lips more, for example brushing against them with a glass, fingers, straw, or their glasses.

- ✔ Their lips look fuller.

- ✔ Their pupils are dilated and their eyes are glassy.

- ✔ They're touching themselves or you more.

- ✔ They're licking or biting their lips.

- ✔ Their feet, hips, and shoulders are all directly aligned with yours. With the exception of full-on flirting, this pose is only adopted if you're about to confront, challenge, or attack someone.

If you can see three of these signs, or, even better, a cluster of four, then pucker up and get in there.

Heading back to theirs

Being caught up in the heat of the moment is delicious, but you should consider several things before heading back to someone else's place.

On a first meeting

You're experiencing love or lust at first sight, they've invited you back to theirs, and you're hot to trot.

Don't be naive or unprepared regarding what could lie in store. You may be enjoying the hottest flirtation you've ever had and, when the hormones kick in, stopping can be difficult. For many people, the thrill of the flirtation lies in the chase; if the chase is short-lived, so may be the relationship. Think twice about whether you want to go full steam ahead now or to build it into a fabulous seduction at a later date. See the safety tips in Chapter 19 before going back to anyone's place.

Wot, no emergency pants!

Dawn was staying with a friend and enjoying a night out on the town. Unfortunately, Dawn's friend vanished with a rugby player, never to return. Dawn stayed in the club waiting for her until last orders. She couldn't find her friend anywhere and didn't have her phone with her; she knew how to get to her house but didn't know the address or have a key to get in. Dawn decided to stay in town and find a hotel but they were all full. A guy she'd been flirting with earlier offered to help out a damsel in distress. He took her back to his hotel room and promised to be on his best behaviour. However, the minute the lights went out he was all over her. After fighting him off for the third time, she headed for the hotel lobby and stayed there until it was light enough to walk to her friend's house.

People don't always behave like they say they're going to, so make sure you have the number of a cab, a means to get in to where you're staying, and plenty of spare cash before you hit the town.

Once you're dating

When you're both ready and your hormones are at boiling point, this is the perfect time to be heading back to theirs. However, if either of you has any doubts, discuss them. Don't push for or be pushed into something that either you or they aren't ready for.

Always carry a condom.

Preparing to Seduce

In the courtship process, just after flirting, but just before sex, comes seduction. Although this book is essentially about flirting, sometimes you can find yourself zipping past it into the realms of seduction, so having the heads up on preparing to seduce is a good move. For more information about getting the sex angle spot on, check out Dr Ruth Westheimer and Pierre Lehu's *Sex For Dummies* (Wiley).

Melting with anticipation

Anticipation is seduction's most vital ingredient. Think back to the strength of your desire for Christmas when you were a child, when you knew that Santa was coming with lots of presents. As an adult you still look forward to receiving presents but not to the same degree. Often the anticipation is better than what you actually get!

Visualisation can be a great aid to anticipation. Imagine where you're going with your date, how good they're going to look and smell, how they'll feel to touch, and how much you're going to enjoy each other's company.

To build your anticipation and theirs, try the following:

✔ Think about how much you're looking forward to seeing your date and how exciting being near them will be.

✔ Send a text telling them why you can't wait to see them and describing what you anticipate happening when you meet.

Making a chemical connection

As well as being physically attracted to someone, if you're also chemically compatible the relationship can ascend dizzying heights. You can enhance this connection with your pheromones, the sex hormones released from the armpit and groin area. *Pheromones* are odourless chemical messengers secreted by animals and humans that the nose picks up at a subconscious level, telling the other person that you're sexually attracted to them.

Discreetly moisten your lips a little before kissing to give your chemical connection a boost. The first kiss has a special purpose. When you're attracted to someone the glands in your mouth and the corners of your lips release *semiochemicals* – the collective name for a number of chemical messages which can facilitate everything from fight or flight to attract or repel responses, and which stimulate sexual desire. People lick their lips not only for auto-erotic purposes but also to prepare the ground for their kissing chemical connections. If the kiss is electric, not only are they a great kisser but you're chemically suited, too.

Being brazen

Being brazen means using your clothes and your attitude to maximise your air of confidence and readiness. At the point where you're past flirting and have seduction on your mind, start to physically reveal more of yourself. Tauten your body posture so that you're showing yourself in your best and most sexy light, and look them right in the eye. When they can see that you so obviously want them, they'll be driven wild with anticipation.

Loosen your shirt, or raise your hemline a little, sit with your legs parted and your chest out, and look them in the eye whilst gently touching yourself, as shown in Figure 13-1.

Figure 13-1: Being brazen.

Becoming Intimate

Unless your relationship ends early or you've both decided not to begin a sexual relationship, you have to decide when to become sexually involved with each other and talk about the associated general issues, such as sexual safety. If you and your partner aren't in agreement about when to begin a sexual relationship, then talking through the issues is important. Good communication is the cornerstone of any relationship and can resolve unnecessary areas of conflict or misunderstanding.

Taking things at your pace

Being yourself is important. If you feel you're being rushed or things are going too slowly, you're not going to appear relaxed and natural.

If you feel you're being pressured into taking things too quickly, for example you're seeing too much of them too soon or feeling pressured into hitting the hay, be honest and tell them that things are going faster than you'd like and set the pace for future relations. A date worth keeping will respect your wishes.

If you're frustrated that things are going too slowly, for example you're only seeing them once in a blue moon or you've been dating for ages and you've only kissed, talk to your date about seeing them more often or ask gently if something's behind their reticence.

Taking precautions

Pregnancy isn't your only worry when starting a sexual relation-ship; you also need to consider sexually-transmitted infections (STIs). According to the Department of Health, STI statistics are at an all-time high and those over the age of 45 are particularly vulnerable.

If you risk having unprotected sex in a casual relationship you're also risking your health.

No contraceptive protects you from everything but a condom is the next best thing. Stick to your guns and make sure you always use a condom until you're in a mutually-exclusive relationship and have established that neither of you has an STI.

Attitudes towards contraception differ depending on what you've been told as a child.

✔ You're not 'easy' because you've had the sense to carry a condom.

✔ Sex isn't 'better' without a condom.

✔ Someone who has had sex with anyone else is a risk to your sexual health if you don't use a condom.

Chapter 14

Considering Dating Rules and Relationship Advice

*W*hether dating friends or colleagues, this territory comes with some caveats to observe before you throw yourself into changing the nature of your relationship, particularly if you want to gain a partner, and not lose a friend.

This chapter covers bagging your dream date so I include some invaluable tips on dating etiquette. For after you've hooked them, I also include some solid advice for making your rosy new relationship bloom.

Starting an Office Romance

Most people meet their future spouse at work, but before you pack in your dating subscription, cancel your speed-dating extravaganza, and wait for the proposals of marriage to flood in, you need to consider a few things.

Getting to know somebody better in the office while under the protective relationship of being a colleague is a fantastic way to decide if you like them without actually showing your hand.

Flirting with married colleagues is one of the worst and potentially most destructive scenarios. When you work at close quarters day in and day out, you get to know each other extremely well. The romance can seem like a match made in heaven. Their partner doesn't understand them and you're a paradise in their otherwise stressful existence – or so they lead you to believe. I guarantee that once they've had their wicked way with you, they'll see no reason to leave their spouse, because they've had their cake and eaten it! Once you start to nag them that you want more of a commitment, you become part of their problem, not their solution.

Factors to consider first

Before approaching a colleague romantically you first need to check out whether the feeling is mutual. If it is, you can tell because they treat you more favourably than other colleagues, pay you more attention, give you lots of eye contact, smile at you more, and so on; if they're not doing this, then discretion and maintaining the relationship as a professional one is better. Check out the signs of mutual interest with a bit of help from Chapter 12.

Another thing to consider is your status in relation to the person you're interested in. Some office relationships are more tolerable than others to the company. The most desirable scenario is if the person is in another department and has a similar status in the company to you.

Relationships between people of unequal status are more problematic. Pursuing someone of lower status can leave you vulnerable to manipulation, so if you're in this situation make it clear that you won't be giving them any preferential treatment. Also, be aware that, if the wheel falls off, the more senior person is the one expected to behave better.

Finally, consider how ending the relationship may affect your work environment. People rarely fall out of love at the same time; friction can be created in the workplace if the person who is most keen to split is being upset by the avid pursuit of the other party. The smooth operation of the company can also be affected if people in the office take sides with the individuals concerned.

Make sure you can transfer elsewhere if the relationship doesn't go to plan. Or, if your company frowns on relationships at work, be prepared to leave the company in order to protect your career prospects and keep your relationship intact.

Office romance etiquette

If you decide to pursue an office romance, follow these rules to minimise the potential for problems and bad feelings with your colleagues:

✔ **Take the relationship at a pace you're happy with, especially if they're senior to you; don't be rushed into anything you're not ready for just because they're higher up the food chain.** They'll respect you more for it and if they don't – ditch them, you've had a lucky escape.

✔ **Keep your decision-making objective.** Having a massive crush on someone isn't the basis for taking their side in an argument and only alienates your colleagues and undermines your reputation.

In instances where it could be deemed that a conflict of interest exists, make sure you declare it to ensure your reputation in the company remains intact.

✔ **Be discreet in the office.** Being caught smooching over the photocopier is never a good career move and is embarrassing for colleagues to witness.

✔ **Don't blab to your colleagues about your date's intimate attributes.** Not only is doing so childish, but if you do end up walking down the aisle you'll wish you'd kept your mouth shut as they're grinning and nudging each other over their hymn sheets.

When you're sure that an office romance is the way forward, try the opening lines for such a scenario in Chapter 16.

Moving from Friends to Lovers

Discovering a friend may actually be dating material is an exciting prospect. Not only do they already know your friends, they're also part of your established social scene and you know their likes and dislikes and they know yours. They may even be known and liked by your family, which is often a hurdle to jump. Making the leap from friends to lovers seems an obvious move once you've considered the consequences.

Just as in any flirting situation, you first need to assess whether the other party shares the interest you feel. Key to consider is whether their behaviour towards you has changed compared to what you're used to experiencing. Consider whether they're spending more time with you, sitting next to you more often, responding more favourably to your comments in a group context, and so on. Head to Chapter 12 for more on the signs of mutual attraction.

If the person you're interested in has a reputation for fishing within the group for dates and then tossing them back once they're bored or a better fish comes along, proceed with caution unless you're happy to be turned into bait.

One to the dog, nil to Jonathan

Jonathan was on a blind date at a dinner party arranged by Julia. He was distracted from his date by Philippa, a newcomer to their social group, and shared a secret smile with her as he discreetly fed the inedible dessert to the dog under the table. The girls in the group were hostile towards unsuspecting Philippa, but on feeling the chill in the air she rebuffed Jonathan's attempts at flirtation. Julia was furious with Jonathan for overlooking her friend, and flirting with Philippa, but not half as outraged as when she found a greasy stain on her carpet and a pile of dog sick in the corner. Jonathan didn't see Julia's friend again but saw Philippa in secret until she had cemented her place in the group and they outed their relationship to everyone's approval.

If you're dating within a group of friends, don't rush straight into things. Think about their feelings first to avoid upsetting the group dynamic.

With a bit of effort, you stand a better chance of forming a lasting relationship with a former friend than from dating a stranger, but are you prepared to lose them as a friend if it doesn't work out? Proceed with caution if not. You don't need to be full on with a friend; excessive contact which isn't returned, or demanding lots of separate date time to your normal social circle, leads them to think you're more like a stalker than a date.

Even if no obvious factors stand in the way of your beautiful friendship turning into a fabulous relationship, be mindful of the feelings of people in the group to maintain the equilibrium of your social circle. Although the vast majority of friends will be delighted that you've paired up, some people are naturally resistant to change; they tend to like things to be the way they've always been. Follow these tips:

- Assure anyone who reacts out of character that things in your group of friends are going to be as good as they've always been.

- Establish if your friends have any particular concerns, for example they feel uncomfortable about you hugging and kissing around them, and modify your behaviour accordingly.

- If you dislike confrontation, ignore your friends' unreasonable antipathy to your relationship. They'll either eventually accept the relationship as it becomes part of the fabric of your group or the matter will come to a head and you'll all be forced to deal with it.

Is there an ex within your social circle? If so, is the ex fine with the new couple dating, or could they be harbouring a grudge or passion for their ex that could disrupt your happy social community? To avoid upset, have a proper conversation with the ex before proceeding.

Getting in the Dating Saddle

When you're flirting like a demon and have your dates on the horizon, use the following tips to make those encounters a success.

Who asks whom?

Who asks for the date can depend on the gender and age of the people involved. Men have traditionally been expected to do the asking and have suffered more from the risk of rejection as a result. Nowadays, the younger the person is, that is, under 30, the less likely this expectation is to be true. For people in their thirties to mid-fifties, asking is a bit of a grey area. Despite decades of equal rights legislation, a minority of women expect to take the upper hand in this age bracket. Women aged over 55 have generally been conditioned into expecting men to do the asking, the inference being that if they take the initiative they'll be considered 'easy'.

Of course, it doesn't really matter who takes the initiative to make the date, so long as one of you does!

Making arrangements

Having all the following questions to hand when arranging your date helps you control your nerves and makes you sound confident and in control.

Deciding on where and when

Decide on the details of the venue, the time, and so on. Find out if your date has any special dietary requirements and take those into consideration. Also determine whether you're going to meet at a certain location or travel there together. (See Chapter 19 for tips on safety.)

 If the person asks you to choose somewhere for your date, don't go for the most expensive place in town, unless they've told you that money is no object. Pick somewhere you know, so that you feel relaxed and can be at your most natural with your date; they'll appreciate your effort.

Nothing but the best!

Phil asked Erica out on a date. He was new to the city and asked her to pick a venue. Erica wanted Phil to think she was classy and not the type of girl accustomed to dining at the lower end of the dining budget, so she picked an expensive new restaurant. She didn't warn Phil about the dress code and at first they couldn't get in because Phil was wearing jeans; with a bit of blagging on Erica's part, however, they were eventually admitted. Erica acted as if dining out in style was part of her daily lifestyle as she knocked back the champagne and chose dishes with the highest price tags. Phil had a marvellous time with his new girl about town and couldn't wait to repeat the experience, a sentiment echoed by Erica until he asked her for her contribution to the rather hefty bill.

Avoid nasty surprises and agree how the bill is going to be paid in advance.

Be sure to trade contact numbers on the day in case of emergencies.

Deciding who pays

Agree in advance who's going to pay. Obviously nowadays it is as acceptable for a man as a woman to pay, or to split the bill. However, attitudes towards footing the bill can be age and gender driven:

- ✔ Sometimes if a woman pays the bill or pays half, she feels she's creating a safety net so that her date won't be expecting anything in return.

- ✔ An older woman may expect a man to pay as an act of chivalry.

- ✔ If you know that your date earns less than you, offering to pay half is polite.

If you want to pay, say you want to treat them when you offer the invitation. Or if they're asking you and you feel more comfortable paying half, say you'd be delighted to accept on the condition you 'go Dutch'. If you're going on a blind date and you don't want to feel any commitment to, or obligation for, a second date, for either party, suggest you split the bill when you're arranging the date. Say 'I normally go Dutch on a blind date, just to avoid any feeling of obligation; is that okay with you?'

Getting the date off to a good start

You can do several things to hit the ground running at the start of your date:

✔ **Aim to be a little early, or at least on time.** Turning up 30 minutes late because you couldn't find a car parking space won't make them feel very special and may get things off to a frosty start.

✔ **Dress to impress and ensure your personal hygiene is flawless.** Looking fantastic but smelling like a goat won't win you a lot of brownie points and makes you memorable for the wrong reasons.

✔ **Start the date with a compliment to boost your date's confidence and set the tone for the evening.** 'I've really been looking forward to seeing/meeting you' or 'You look great' are good beginners because they're simple, easy to deliver, and easy to respond to.

Compliments are a great and effective way to make your date think you like them, and dates are much more likely to like people whom they think like them.

Being honest and presenting a reliable impression of yourself is vital on your first date, rather than trying to be what you guess your date's looking for. Building your relationship from a position of trust leads to a solid bond; false starts can create doubts that may be difficult or impossible to overcome.

Good manners and civility cost nothing; don't forget to thank your date for their time, company, and generosity (if they've paid).

Knowing when to call after the date

Different schools of thought exist on when to call following a date, ranging from 'treat them mean and keep them keen' to playing coy. Your main aim, however, is to let your date know how you felt about your meeting, whether you're interested, or thanks but no thanks.

Phoning, emailing, and texting are perfectly acceptable ways of contacting your date, provided you make your intention clear.

Telling someone who's over-keen, when the feeling isn't mutual, that you'd like to see them again 'at some point in the future when you have less time commitments', may seem like a polite way to fob them off but is actually allowing them to maintain hope. They'll keep calling until your fictitiously full diary can accommodate them or until you're forced to be honest with them.

Cyber stalking

Lisa's first date with David went fantastically well. Glowing with enthusiasm, she texted him from the taxi home. Although he didn't respond, the thought of David kept her awake with visions of holidays, marriage, and babies. David still hadn't contacted her by lunchtime the next day, so Lisa assumed he had a problem with his phone and started emailing him. A week and a mountain of emails later, David still hadn't surfaced. She hunted him down on Facebook, but still he didn't respond. Eventually Lisa had to face up to the reality that David was avoiding her and perhaps her courtship was more akin to cyber stalking than a gentle hint that she was attracted to him.

Accept that not all dates lead to something more. If they don't respond within a reasonable length of time, walk away and concentrate on flirting with someone completely different.

Texting, phoning, leaving answerphone messages, or emailing to say that you've 'had a great time and would like to see them again if the feeling is mutual' is a very clear and concise way of letting them know you like them and you'd like to repeat the experience. If they haven't responded within 48 hours, trying once more is permissible; any longer and they clearly aren't going to.

Research shows that men tend not to consider time in relation to returning a date's calls, whereas women dwell on it. He'll call you when he's ready and won't understand why you're huffy that he's left it until the following week.

Include a compliment about your date when you first respond. A simple 'I really enjoyed your company' suffices.

Going from Dating to a Relationship

Initially in the dating process, seeing more than one person is perfectly acceptable (do make sure that all parties are aware of this situation, though!). Eventually, however, you need to decide which person you want to continue in a relationship with. When you see that your feelings are being reciprocated, be honest about your intentions and communicate clearly. Remember, lasting relationships stem from great communication, regardless of whether they're dates, friends, or colleagues.

Discovering whether someone is as enamoured of you as you are of them isn't always as straightforward as it sounds. Circumstances masking how much of a mutual attraction exists (or doesn't) include people doing the following:

✔ Sending the wrong signals

✔ Not being able to read the signals you're sending out

✔ Not being honest about their feelings for fear of rejection

✔ Not expressing themselves clearly

For these people, establishing whether you're out of dating territory and into a relationship is going to take time. Don't wear your heart on your sleeve, but be candid; if the feeling's mutual, it helps your date to open up.

 Working out if they're 'the one' and you can stop flirting for dates can be a challenge. Some people set such high expectations for relationships that they're doomed to a lifetime of looking and feeling short-changed. But if you're realistic and pragmatic about love, you may realise that 'this is it' right in front of you.

Knowing if you're in it for the long term

Sharing similar values and beliefs is the basis of a great long-term relationship. Ask yourself if you:

✔ Want similar lifestyles, for example type of home, pets, work–life balance.

✔ Both want children, and when, how many, and so on.

✔ Have a similar approach to work and careers, that is, working to live or living to work.

✔ Share the same attitudes toward family and friends, for example the amount of time you want to spend with them and how much you value them.

✔ Enjoy similar leisure and holiday activities.

✔ Have the same attitude toward spirituality, for example you're both atheist or share a compatible religion.

Clearly, if he's a mummy's boy workaholic who doesn't want kids, hates DIY, and doesn't know one end of a lawnmower from the other, and you have an aversion to in-laws, a love of house renovation, a ticking body clock, and a two-acre lawn, the relationship's not going to last.

Opposites do attract, but having values and beliefs in common provides a better basis for a future together.

Managing minor irritations

Nobody's perfect, not even you, so give and take are important in a relationship. Once you accept that a completely perfect mate doesn't exist but you've found one who's pretty close, you just need to manage the things you find less desirable about them to keep your relationship ticking along nicely.

If they really can't change the things that annoy you about them, it becomes your problem not theirs, and you have to find a way to deal with it before it becomes a wedge between you.

Don't make all the minor irritations a battleground. Save the arguments for the really important stuff. When something annoys you, completely ignore it.

Sharing a little love every day

Never take for granted that somebody knows how you feel about them. To build a strong relationship, get into the habit of showing and telling them you love them every day. Family and close friends also need love, so show them, too.

Physical contact is very important for human beings. Give them a hug when they don't expect it and a little kiss when you're passing to keep your physiological bond strong.

Chapter 15

Reducing the Risk of Rejection

● ●

In This Chapter

▶ Picking the right people to flirt with

▶ Managing risk by degrees

▶ Salvaging a flirtation

▶ Dealing with rejection

● ●

*A*ll of us experience fear at some time; if we didn't, we'd be oblivious to danger. However, developing an overly sensitive fear of rejection can have a detrimental impact upon your life and your ability to form and build relationships. While nobody likes to feel, or be, rejected, everyone experiences it at one time or another.

Perspective is something we tend to lose when dealing with rejection; however, it can be a great friend to your ego and help you to learn from and overcome rejection much faster. Even better than perspective is risk assessment, because it actively helps you avoid the risk of rejection and make better choices in the first place. In this chapter, you discover how to minimise the risk of rejection by making good choices of who to flirt with in the first place, stretching your comfort zone by taking risks, and equally as importantly learning how to handle rejection with dignity and confidence.

Gaining Some Perspective on Rejection

Fear of rejection can manifest itself in many different ways. You may tell yourself 'I can't do this' or 'I'm hopeless at doing that' or 'They won't like me, so I won't bother even trying'.

Fear of rejection can often stem from an earlier rejection, possibly from your very first attempt at a meaningful flirtation with someone you found really attractive, when your hormones were racing, and the outcome was the biggest thing ever to have happened in your short life. Being rejected felt devastating. The shock and disappointment of this event may have made you avoid being in a position of risking such hurt and humiliation ever again.

To put this rejection into perspective, it probably happened when you were at the very beginning of your flirting journey, before you'd developed all the lovely flirting skills that Mother Nature blessed you with and which are outlined in this book. You were at your least well-equipped to tell if you should've risked flirting with this person and whether they were interested in you in the first place. Actually, this rejection was an essential part of your flirting learning process.

You've carried this fear of rejection with you ever since and it surfaces when you find yourself in an unfamiliar situation or when meeting new people. Even though facing genuine danger is unlikely, you're still frightened by something that takes you out of your comfort zone.

Rejection strikes right to the very core of you and feels like a personal slight. Actually, though, someone may reject you for a myriad of reasons; many of them either out of your control or nothing to do with you. The person could already be in a relationship, not looking for a relationship, be painfully shy and fearful of rejection themselves, be having a night out with friends and not on the pull, or have just emerged from a messy breakup – the list is endless.

Making the Right Initial Choices: A Flirting Checklist

Choosing to flirt with someone you find attractive, as opposed to someone who's available, is a very common mistake and one of the main reasons for rejection. Yet the person being rejected takes it personally, even when the object of their failed flirtation wasn't looking for someone to flirt with in the first place. You can minimise your chances of rejection at the early stages of a flirtation by working through the flirting checklist and making sure everyone's getting the right message.

History repeating itself

Mark had an abysmal track record of flirting with women. None of them seemed to like him and he'd written himself off as a hopeless flirt, so sick of knock-backs he'd vowed never to approach a strange woman again. Actually, Mark was quite able to flirt with women who approached him. It transpired that his rejection was simply down to picking women who were either out with their boyfriends or not interested in flirting.

Mark had to work quite hard at learning how to tell who was available for flirting, but once he cracked it, his flirting success rate was nearly 100 per cent.

Don't write yourself off due to fear of rejection; the problem probably lies elsewhere.

The flirting checklist can be broken down into three points: being able to judge whether they're available, sending the right signals to show you're interested, and being able to assess the other person's response. To avoid picking someone who isn't available for a flirtation, so minimising the risk of rejection, keep these points in mind.

Are they available?

You can tell whether someone's available for a flirtation by paying attention to their body language and position in the room. Look for the following:

- ✔ Are they scanning the room looking to see who's available?

- ✔ If they're standing with other people, are they facing the busy part of the room?

- ✔ Are they showing any classic male/female preening gestures such as smoothing down his tie or lapel, touching his face, lip licking, or playing with or tossing their hair (see Chapter 12 for a more complete list)?

If the answer is yes to all three questions, you can safely assume that they're looking.

Giving signs that I like them

When you've established that someone is available for a flirtation, you need to make sure you send the right signals demonstrating that you're interested (and receive the right response, as I explain in the next section) before you proceed.

Have you given them:

- ✔ A chance to get the best view of you; that is, have you moved to the most advantageous spot in the room? You can find more on choosing power spots in Chapter 7.

- ✔ The right flirting body language pose for your gender? Ladies, you can make yourself curvier and guys can stand with a wider leg stance. Chapter 12 gives you the lowdown.

- ✔ A four-second glance? Look at them for four seconds, look away, and then look back. If they're still looking, they're interested. Chapter 10 has more about mastering the four-second glance.

- ✔ An eyebrow flash? A quick up–down of the eyebrows to say a non-verbal hello goes a long way. Chapter 7 tells you more.

- ✔ A smile? If they smile back you can take it as a very positive sign. Chapter 10 goes into more detail about what's in a smile.

Sending all these signals makes it clear to the other person that you want to start flirting with them.

Are they responding?

Before you proceed, you need to confirm that the response you're getting is one that encourages your flirtation. Has the person you're about to flirt with:

- ✔ Moved to get a better look at you?
- ✔ Returned eye contact?
- ✔ Flashed you back?
- ✔ Smiled back?
- ✔ Used any gender-specific flirting signals (see Chapter 12)?

If they've demonstrated at least three of these five signals you can assume they're interested in starting a flirtation with you and you've minimised the risk of rejection at this stage.

Taking Acceptable Risks

Nothing in life is without risk, but once you convince yourself that you've weighed everything up and you've got more to gain than

to lose, you're taking an acceptable risk, which is so much easier.
Different levels of risk are incurred at each stage of the flirting
process:

✔ **Stage 1:** Deciding who to flirt with is the least risky in terms of
rejection.

✔ **Stage 2:** Deciding who to strike up a conversation with is
slightly more risky.

✔ **Stage 3:** Making a pass at someone is the most risky, but
compared to other personal risks you take, such as driving or
flying, is very small.

Who to flirt with

The more experience you have at flirting, the more likely you are
to be prepared to take risks to initiate a flirtation. The first part of
the flirting process is non-verbal, so you're risking virtually nothing by having a go.

How big a risk you're taking depends on whom you're initiating a
flirtation with:

✔ **Virtually rejection risk free:** Friends and family.

✔ **Slight risk:** Colleagues and strangers.

✔ **Slightly more risky:** People you're strongly attracted to.

Even the riskiest category – people you're strongly attracted to –
doesn't pose much of a risk. The worst that can happen is that
someone doesn't return your glance, eyebrow flash, or smile. This
scenario isn't the end of the world; you haven't suffered any huge
personal rejection. You have nothing to lose.

Build up your comfort zone by non-verbally flirting your way
through the different levels of risk.

Striking up a conversation

Having conquered your fear of rejection for the first stages of non-
verbal flirting (see the preceding section) and realised that nothing
terrible happened as a result, you're ready to overcome the fear
of rejection whilst starting up a conversation. Chapter 16 provides
a list of safe opening lines, so you have nothing to stop you from
making the first move to chat.

Life just passing her by

Julie had never had much confidence; she always assumed that people would rather not talk to her, even on mundane subjects. The thought of speaking to a stranger, never mind flirting with one, filled her with horror. She knew they wouldn't like her and would definitely not want to talk to her, so why set herself up for rejection? Julie had thought negatively for so long that her thinking was completely twisted. She kept her head down and avoided even making eye contact as she got on with life.

Julie was persuaded that judging which people wanted to talk to her was possible. She gradually learned to make eye contact, and from that vantage point she could look for the other signs. Life didn't seem quite so daunting now she had a plan to follow. She worked on her interactions with the people she saw on a regular basis and then with the odd dog-walking stranger. Eventually, she had the confidence to pick a man to flirt with. To her amazement, her approach worked a treat. She limited her initial flirting to eye contact and smiling when she saw him in the queue in the sandwich shop; the following day she asked about his choice of filling; and finally, a few weeks later, she asked him to join her for lunch in the park.

Julie's confidence has grown exponentially and her constant fear of rejection is a distant memory. As long as she can weigh up the risk beforehand, she's happy to flirt with everyone, from colleagues to potential dates, at her own pace.

The only valid reasons why someone wouldn't respond to you after your successful non-verbal flirt are that they either didn't hear you or don't speak your language. Any other reason that pops into your head is of your own making and isn't a valid excuse to avoid talking to them. If they turn out to be spoken for or are in a hurry to get back to the office because their boss has just texted them, they'll still respond to you, even if just to say hello and to make their excuses, but they won't ignore you.

Making a pass at someone

Risking a non-verbal flirt and having a chat are easy once you've overcome your initial fear. Some people, however, feel that making a pass is declaring their hand.

Fear is only present when you allow your mind to think negative thoughts. Focusing on positive thoughts about the feeling of success that follows successfully pulling a date instills a sense of confidence and gives you a positive outlook.

Reassure yourself that they've accepted your non-verbal flirtation and have enjoyed talking with you. They're giving off the right signals and waiting for you to make the next move.

If you're receiving the signals that the other person is game (refer to Chapter 12) and they've been present or increasing since you started talking, strike while the iron's hot.

Action defeats fear. Taking action means you don't have time to ponder on your fear of rejection, which, ultimately, paralyses you into doing nothing and makes your fear a self-fulfilling prophecy. So, whether you want their telephone number, a date, or a kiss, trust your instincts and make your move.

Write yourself a pulling mantra and repeat it to yourself several times a day. Say it like you mean it and crack your fear of rejection.

Getting Things Back on Track

Flirtations can be quashed and rejection caused by anything from coffee breath to standing too close to the other person to them worrying about being perceived as unprofessional if you're flirting at work. If you really fancy them, seeing what you can do to salvage the situation is worthwhile.

To try to get things back on track, follow these steps:

1. **Think back to the point at which things started to cool off.**

   What were you both saying or doing at the time? Can you identify what in particular may have been the trigger for the turn?

   Think about the circumstances and context of your flirtation, too. Flirting's likely to go better in an environment where this behaviour's acceptable – a bar compared to an office, for example. Also consider if the other person's circumstances have recently changed; if they've been made redundant, been promoted, or dumped by a lover, they may feel more or less flirtatious than usual.

2. **Give them a bit more space.**

   If you feel a flirtation's going off the boil, giving them some space is the best approach. Don't be tempted to crowd them, as you damage your chances of retrieving the situation.

3. **Mention that they seem to have changed since whatever you think the turning point is and ask them if anything's wrong.**

   If doing so clears the air, either carry on with your flirtation or consider meeting at another time. If they're vague and you don't feel as though they've given you an answer, they're probably not for you. Make your excuses and leave.

Your move, Mike

Mike had no problem meeting and chatting to girls. However, his friends were curious as to why he never seemed to have a girlfriend. It was only when one friend gently tried to coax him out of the closet that he confessed his single status was nothing to do with his sexuality. He just couldn't make the transition from flirting to going out with a woman. He couldn't be sure that they actually fancied him and was terrified of being rejected. As a result, girls eventually became friends or lost interest in waiting for him to make a move.

Mike wrote himself a flirting mantra to boost his confidence and overcome his fear of rejection: 'I'm smart, sexy, and funny; she wants me!' He said it to himself every day in the shower and when he was getting ready for a night out. Finally, he used it in action. He was well into a flirtation and reached the point at which he normally flunked it. Instead of holding off, he mentally chanted his mantra and asked a woman for her phone number. A few months later, when he was confident about that stage, he worked on asking women for a date there and then. After that he conquered recognising the stage at which a woman wanted to be kissed.

Before he knew it, Mike had a reputation as a ladies' man and decided that he was ready to find the right girl.

Don't let your fear of rejection ruin your chances of a relationship. Push your comfort zone until you've stretched it enough to make a pass at someone without fear.

Handling Rejection

Life's about taking occasional risks and, even though that means letting yourself flirt with the unknown, you need to approach any new experience or challenge with the courage and determination to succeed.

You may not succeed all of the time but by adopting a healthy attitude to success and realising that sometimes you'll make mistakes along the way, you can view flirting failures as chances to learn from experience. Ultimately, you reach your flirting goal.

Make any rejection work for you by not dwelling on it, but turning it into a positive learning experience. The way you handle rejection says a lot about you as a person.

Rejection isn't personal; it's just life's selection process. Whether you're doing the rejecting or are on the receiving end of it, it's part and parcel of dating. Getting rejection out of the way without fuss or recrimination is best for everyone concerned.

When you're doing the rejecting

If you're the one doing the rejecting, start giving them the message by cutting down on all the body language signals that you like them – lessen eye contact, smile less, and move further away from them (explained in Chapter 11) – and on the secret flirting signals – less hair play, preening, and so on (discussed in Chapter 12). Doing so should be enough to alert them to the fact that your flirtation has come to an end.

Thankfully this is enough to give most people the message. However, if they still don't get it you need to spell it out to them in the most low-key way possible. Keep your composure, so as not to excite them into a debate over it, and calmly explain that it's unfortunate but they're not your type, and that you don't get to find these things out without giving it a go first. Chapter 18 can give you more advice here.

Telling someone why you don't like them may be spoiling for a fight. Avoid saying things such as 'You're not my type because you're too short, tall, fat, noisy, quiet, unattractive'. Personal comments aren't necessary; the person has nothing wrong with them, they're just not the right one for you. Avoid a scene and stick to neutral comments.

Turning the rejection to the other person's advantage is a better solution; try 'It's been nice to meet you, but I don't think I'm the right person for you. I'll get out of your hair now to leave the way clear for Mr/Mrs Right.' You're actually doing them a favour by telling them not to waste any more time or effort on you.

Avoid ditching them in front of their friends, because nothing's more likely to cause a scene than someone jumping to defend their friend's honour.

When you're being rejected

If someone's told you that you're not for them, accept their decision.

Now is not the time to ask them 20 questions to justify why they don't want to carry on the flirtation. Even if they did give you a justification, you're unlikely to change their mind with any of your responses. The time to challenge their thinking was when their body language started going off track (as Chapter 11 explains). Trying to remedy the situation now is too late.

Be grateful that they've been honest with you and not left you hanging on expectantly for a relationship that was never going to materialise.

Moving on graciously increases the speed at which you're likely to meet someone more worthy of your flirtation. Don't waste time hovering around the person trying to change their mind.

Managing rejection at work

Possibly the worst place to be rejected by someone is at work, because you're likely to bump into them regularly; if you're in the same department, you'll have to deal with seeing them every day.

However the rejection manifests itself or who is responsible for it, take the initiative and clear the air before it affects your working relationships and career prospects.

How you're seen to be managing rejection can have a big impact on your reputation, so aim to manage it with dignity. Meet them (or send them an email if you can't get a quiet word) and say, 'Just to clear the air, I feel it didn't work out between us. It's no reflection on you; we're just not right for each other. However, I don't want this to spoil our professional relationship and I'll be making every effort to ensure things are fine between us at work. I hope you share this sentiment.' Or, if you're the one who's been rejected, simply say 'I don't want what's happened to spoil our professional relationship, and I hope our working relationship will continue to thrive without this impacting on it'.

Lynn's way and the wrong way

Lynn was quite adept at chatting to men but was a bit overpowering, especially when she'd had a drink. Actually, she wasn't every man's cup of tea. She didn't take the hint and would follow the men she fancied round and round until they had to tell her in no uncertain terms that they weren't interested. She'd then interrogate them about why they didn't fancy her. When they told her, she'd be indignant and argue with them in a bid to get them to retract their rejection and agree with her on their suitability as a couple. If they still wouldn't agree, she'd drag their friends into the argument, until it all got very messy and unpleasant. After some flirting coaching Lynn learned to see rejection as a lucky escape and the opportunity to move on to Mr Right. She also cut back on the amount she was drinking and put more effort into reading the body language signals that let her know how someone felt about her, rather than relying on booze to do the talking. Her friends commented on how much more fun she was to go out with and her reputation as an aggressive man-eater faded away.

Learn to graciously accept someone's decision to discontinue the flirtation with you to minimise the trauma associated with rejection.

Now you're redundant, now you're not!

Stefan had been selected for redundancy by his company and met with his managing director to discuss the terms. Although the company was going through a consultation process with the staff about how the redundancies could be avoided, they were pretty much a done deal. During the course of the meeting, however, the MD was so impressed with Stefan's dignity and his gratitude for the opportunities he'd experienced with the company that he decided Stefan had a side that he hadn't yet had the chance to experience and qualities that he was unaware of. He decided it would be a mistake to let Stefan go, based on his reaction to the news of his redundancy, and kept him on in a newly created and more senior post.

Accepting rejection with dignity can pay off, even when you think you have nothing to gain by it.

Never chat about rejecting someone at work. Office gossip will circulate the story in no time and it'll probably bear little resemblance to your original version of events.

Part V
The Part of Tens

"I've been told I have the worst opening line in the world. But not Mr. Moppet..."

In this part . . .

This part provides a light-hearted look at opening lines, things to avoid when flirting, strategies for getting rid of unwanted attention, and essential tips to make sure you flirt safely.

Chapter 16

Ten (Or So) Opening Lines for Almost Any Occasion

*G*enerally, what you say is less important than how you say it. Even so, having something to say is always handy, so you can focus your energy on looking and sounding confident and not worry about conversational gaffes!

This chapter offers some stock opening lines to use in a range of situations, so you have no excuse not to approach someone and get stuck into your flirting. All these lines are much more effective when you use them along with the tips elsewhere in the book. If you're lucky, the recipient may even have read this book too and recognise from your opening line that you're initiating a flirtation!

Don't forget your closing line is just as important as your opening line. If you realise that you've made a terrible mistake and you can't get rid of the person, check out Chapter 18 for some tips. Otherwise, you can just say 'It's been really lovely to meet you; perhaps I'll bump into you later.' or 'Here's my number, give me a call sometime; it would be great to hear from you.'

Opening Lines for Men

Men often feel under tremendous pressure to deliver the perfect witty opening line. The truth is, women fall in love with their ears. After they get past the initial attraction, it's what they hear and how you make them feel about themselves that counts. You can do well here by paying compliments – women need to know that you like them.

Try these opening lines (make eye contact and wear a friendly expression):

✔ **'If you don't mind me saying, you've got the nicest smile/ loveliest eyes/most wicked laugh/best perfume in the room.'** This is a good line if you're feeling confident; it works because you've asked permission to speak to her and paid her a compliment.

✔ **'You look like a nice, friendly person so I thought I'd come and say hello. I'm X and I'm pleased to meet you.'** Remember to finish this line off with an offer of a handshake. This is a good one if you're new to opening lines. It works because you've paid her a general compliment and then got your first bit of intentional touching (the handshake) in, which boosts your confidence and creates a positive and lasting effect. Also, conversational etiquette dictates that she'll offer her name and handshake in return. If her name and handshake are not immediately forthcoming, the natural progression for your next line is, 'What's your name?'

Opening Lines for Women

Men are generally so delighted that they're not doing the running that you can say pretty much anything and not worry about being rejected. Women tend to use indirect opening lines rather than the obvious chat up, for example 'Do you have the time?', 'I'm not from round here; can you recommend a decent restaurant?', 'I'm trying to avoid that man over there; could you do me a favour and engage in animated conversation with me for a minute, please?'

Deliver indirect opening lines while offering the female flirting clues (covered in Chapter 12) to avoid being given a straight answer. Here, you're creating the opportunity to flirt rather than initiating it. To leap straight into flirting, try these lines:

✔ **'Great shirt/tie/aftershave, where did you get it from?'** This works as an opening line because you've appealed to his ego by complimenting his choice, and, because men are factually orientated, he'll be happy to discuss where the item came from.

✔ **'Hi, I'm looking for a friendly face to chat to and yours looks friendly to me.'** This works as an opening line because he hasn't had to deliver it and you're expressly letting him know that you like his appearance and want to chat.

Opening Lines for an Office Romance

Don't wait for the Christmas party for the opportunity to get your office romance started. Two types of opening line are useful for office romances: one for using when you think someone has been checking you out and one for when you're making a move on the other person. Try the following:

- ✔ 'I couldn't help but notice that you've been paying me more attention; shall we grab a coffee and have a proper chat?'

- ✔ 'I'm making a point of getting to know more people; do you fancy grabbing a coffee to get the ball rolling?'

These lines work because they're direct and they lead to an invitation.

Opening Lines for Complete Strangers

Your mother may have told you never to speak to strangers, but you're going to have to break childhood habits or risk missing out on spontaneous flirting opportunities. As a starter, talking about the circumstance you both find yourself in is the best strategy with strangers.

'Do you come here often?' works brilliantly if you're in long or slow-moving queues. You break the ice with humour and provide the other person with an easy opportunity to respond.

'Great weather for the time of year.' is another safe positive opener that you can deliver with a smile. People are happy to respond to weather questions and aren't threatened by them, and you can lead easily on to a range of other topics.

If the stranger has a child or dog with them, try complimenting their good behaviour (provided that the child or dog is actually being well behaved!). People like nothing more than speaking about their children or pets.

Opening Lines for Networking

Networking makes most people as nervous as chatting up strangers in a bar. However, with a bit of perseverance, you can overcome the sense of dread and may even come to enjoy the opportunity to form relationships with like-minded people. Try these lines:

- ✔ **'Hi, I'm X, do you mind if I join you?'** This works because you're asking their permission.

- ✔ **'Hi, I'm X, what do (peer at name badge for title of company) you do at company Y, then?'** This works because people love the sound of their own voice and talking about themselves.

Opening Lines for Making Friends

Perhaps you've seen someone around for ages, but only to smile at; you don't know how to introduce yourself or get things on to a friendlier footing. Actually, changing an acquaintance into a friend is easy. Try these lines:

- ✔ **'I feel like I've known you for ages, but realise I don't know your name. I'm X, who are you?'** This works because they probably don't know your name either and it gives you both the excuse to come clean and move your relationship onto a new footing.

- ✔ **'We keep bumping into each other here. Do you fancy getting together some time over coffee and having a proper conversation? If you'd like to give me your number, I'll contact you to fix something up.'** This works because nobody likes to make the first move. They'll be flattered that you asked and if you've met them a few times already, they won't be worried that you may turn out to be a clinger-on.

Opening Lines for Internet Dating

Not having to deliver it in person is the best thing about your opening line for Internet dating. If you want to ooze charm like James Bond but your delivery is more Mr Bean, this is your opportunity to pull it off!

Because the recipient can't hear the intonation in your voice, words and humour really are crucial for Internet dating. Tailor your response to the style of ad they've written and use similar themes, for example:

✔ If she's asked for a 'Knight in shining armour', you could respond: 'Armour currently at drycleaners. Steed did bunk, but have borrowed pit pony in anticipation of transport required to rescue maiden in distress.' This works because you've followed her theme and added your own twist, which gives her something to play with when she continues your online conversation.

✔ If, like me, you're dyslexic and find your spelling a bit embarrassing, you could make light of it by writing: 'Dyslexic cyber dater seeks hot date complete with chell specker.' This works because you're not being self-effacing but are letting them know you have a problem with words. Revealing something personal about yourself allows the other person to respond in kind and immediately moves the interaction on a notch.

Opening Lines for Speed-dating

Speed-dating's great as you're all in the same boat. Everyone knows that everyone else is single and looking for lurve. The pressure's certainly on to find an opening line that works.

You can play it straight or make a remark about the event itself. Here are some examples:

✔ (Playing it straight.) **'Hi, I'm Elizabeth, pleased to meet you'** **followed by a friendly handshake.** This works because standard conversation code is followed and everybody knows where they are and how to respond. (Chapter 8 has more on conversation code.)

✔ (Making a remark about the event.) You can have a lot of fun with this one:

> **'I'm a newcomer to speed-dating, so be gentle with me.'**

> **'Don't you feel like you're in *Groundhog Day*, sitting down to a new face and introducing yourself every few minutes?'**

> **'Making conversation at these things is a bit like having short-term memory loss. I'm never sure if I'm repeating myself in the same conversation!'** (Don't use this line on the first date of the evening, because they'll think you're a crazy person.)

These lines work because you're commenting on a shared experience and making it easy for the other person to respond.

Which one would you be?

One cheesy speed-dater opened every conversation with exactly the same line: 'So, if you were a character from *Friends*, which one would you be and why?', delivered with a raised eyebrow and a leer. You could see the women wince every time he uttered it. At half time, word about Mr Creepy spread in the Ladies and those that were still to meet him armed themselves in preparation.

'Monica, because I'd have no qualms about telling you to get lost,' one woman blurted out before he'd even got a chance to deliver his opening gambit. Then she stood up and swanned off to the bar.

Throughout the evening, people who went for the obvious but simple opening lines faired far better than the ones trying to be clever. Aim for something simple, and within your delivery capabilities, to get the easiest conversations going.

Opening Lines for the Supermarket

Flirting with people in supermarkets is super easy because you can tell so much about them from their food choices. In fact, if they've got a trolley full of fast food and booze you may even want to eliminate them from your flirtation on the grounds that they'll have blocked arteries and a hardened liver before they hit middle age!

The contents of someone's trolley or the waiting time at the checkouts are perfect subjects for opening lines:

- ✔ **'Lychees! I've always wondered what you do with those. Do you have a good recipe for them?'** This works because you're providing a nice safe invitation for them to share their culinary experience with you, or confess they haven't got a clue what to do with them either!

- ✔ **'If I had a penny for every minute I've spent loitering in these checkout queues, I'd be able to shop at Waitrose. Do you come here often?'** This works because you're commenting on a mutual experience, showing a sense of humour, and asking them a question in return to get the conversation started.

- ✔ **'Shopping for one? Me too, do you fancy a coffee in the supermarket cafe after?'** Taking the bull by the horns works because you've identified that they're single (or if they're not, it gives them a chance to say so), and the supermarket's a neutral, noncommittal place to get to know each other a little bit better.

Make someone's day by getting your opening line in first – and you may go home with more than your shopping!

Opening Lines for a Holiday Romance

You don't have a holiday every day, so make the most of it. Holiday romances are great because if you eventually can't stand the sight of them, you won't have to worry about bumping into them or keeping in touch!

- ✔ **'That tan's coming along well'** is particularly effective if they're lobster red or ghostly white. This works well if the person has a sense of humour – if not, you've had a lucky escape!

- ✔ **'What's your favourite place to eat around here?'** This works because you're offering a non-threatening, rejection-free opening line. You can judge by their response if you can move the conversation on to something more flirtatious (see Chapter 8 on working out if someone wants to talk to you).

People are more relaxed on holiday, have more of a sense of humour, and are much more receptive to opening lines – unless they're accompanied by their spouse!

Chapter 17

Ten Flirting Gaffes

This book covers everything you need to know to be the perfect flirt. Sometimes, though, the things you shouldn't be doing are equally important to perfecting your flirting game. Don't dwell on the points listed, simply make a mental note to avoid them (especially if you can recall doing any of them!) and keep on with all the good stuff in the rest of the book. As entertaining as some of the points are, I promise they're all true and have happened to some poor soul in the past.

Saying the Wrong Things to a Woman

'Sorry, it was rude to ask your age. My mother always said you should never ask a woman her age; so what do you weigh, then?' These memorable lines stopped even me in my tracks.

Guys, the following are things you should never say to a woman:

✔ **'You remind me of my mother/sister/favourite female friend/ex.'** Every woman wants to feel unique.

✔ **'You look different, have you put on weight?'** No woman wants to hear this line, for obvious reasons – but feel free to ask if the opposite is true.

✔ **'How old are you? You look different in your picture.'** You'll never work your way back from this one.

✔ **'Your friend is very attractive.'** She'll smile and agree, but on the inside she's seething. Not only have you ruined your chances with her, you'll never get near her mate either.

Saying the Wrong Things to a Man

Certain lines, unless uttered by the man himself, curtail a relationship very quickly. When you're still at the flirting stage, avoid the following until he mentions them:

✔ 'I'd really like you to meet my parents.'

✔ 'If we had kids together, do you think they'd have your eyes?'

✔ 'I'd love to spend all my free time with you.'

✔ 'You make great husband material.'

✔ 'Do you think you'd prefer a wife that doesn't work?'

✔ 'Do I look fat in this?'

✔ 'Do you think that woman over there is attractive?'

✔ 'How much do you love me?'

Until you've been dating for a while, you're unlikely to: (a) get a straight answer or (b) like the response if he's honest.

Delving into Taboo Topics on a First Date

Never mind sex, religion, and politics, the following subjects are absolute no no's on a first date:

✔ **Your ex.** Whether your ex was fabulously good or bad, your date wants to hear about this person about as much as they want a hole in the head.

✔ **Your plans for marriage and children.** This is a first date, not a life sentence.

✔ **How you once poisoned the pet of someone who upset you.** Your date will be contacting the RSPCA whilst escaping out of the toilet window.

Stick to the safe stuff mentioned in Chapters 8 and 9 to make your conversation run smoothly and your rapport build to a gentle crescendo.

Writing Things You'll Regret on the Internet

Never write anything on the Internet unless you're sure you can retract it. Consider having the following details available in perpetuity for all to read and to your eternal embarrassment:

- ✔ How many people you've slept with.
- ✔ The nasty tricks you've played on your boss/ex/best friend.
- ✔ How much you earn.
- ✔ Anything that isn't true.

 Never write anything on the Internet that could lead to your identity being stolen or your house being broken into while you're away.

Picking a Bad Time to Ask for a Date

Timing is everything when asking for a date. Avoid the following situations unless you're prepared for a knock back.

Never ask for a date when:

- ✔ They've just told you their cat or favourite relative has died.
- ✔ They've declared that they still have feelings for their ex.
- ✔ They've spent ten minutes telling you how busy they're going to be for the rest of the year.
- ✔ They've just told you that you're not their type.

You may only get one chance to ask this person out so make sure your timing's perfect.

Botching Up Who Pays the Bill

Paying the bill can be a contentious area, so never assume that your date is a mind reader and has figured out what the score is when it comes to this part of your evening. To avoid creating a scene and jeopardising future dates, never:

✓ Push the bill across the table and announce that it's their turn to pay.

✓ Get your calculator out and split the bill according to what each of you ate, even if you did choose the veggie option and didn't drink.

✓ Offer to split the bill with them, when it was you who invited them out to dinner in the first place.

Agree in advance how you'll handle bills to avoid causing embarrassment and ruining what could've been a beautiful relationship.

Choosing the Wrong Venue

The choice of venue can make or break a date. Play it safe on the first date and avoid places:

✓ Where you can't pronounce the items on the menu.

✓ Serving up animals that people pay money to visit in zoos.

✓ Where you have to shout above the music to make conversation.

✓ That are so brightly lit you need sunglasses.

✓ Where you have to sit and be ignored on a tiny table near the kitchen door unless you're a household name.

Choose somewhere atmospheric, not too quiet, and busy. If you run out of conversation the background noise will fill the silence, and you can always make small talk about the other patrons.

Overreacting to Accidents

In a perfect world no accidents – big or small – would occur on a first date. Unfortunately, because you're in a heightened state of anxiety, you're more likely to be clumsy and have an accident or be more sensitive to things going wrong. To be on the safe side, don't:

✓ Blame your date for the incident; even if they did set fire to the curtains whilst playing carelessly with the candle.

✓ Call your mum, because she always knows what to do in a crisis.

✓ Apologise profusely, even if the incident's not your fault, and state that things always go wrong if you're involved. Nobody wants to go out with a doom monger.

Making a drama out of a crisis isn't necessary. Just ignore whatever's happened and don't make a fuss. You don't want to make your date uncomfortable, nor do you want them to think that you're accident-prone.

Bumping into the Ex

Meeting an ex unexpectedly can really throw you, not to mention your date. Regardless of whether you parted badly, on great terms, or had a one-sided breakup, avoid the following if you want the meeting to pass without incident or repercussion:

- ✔ Introducing them to your new date as the fiancé(e) that got away.

- ✔ Bragging to your ex about how much better your new date is than they ever were.

- ✔ Starting a row, even if they did steal your favourite Spice Girls album and never returned the electric screwdriver they borrowed.

- ✔ Greeting them with a kiss on both cheeks and reminiscing about all the fun times you had together.

Looking Over Their Shoulder

Nobody feels they're the centre of your universe and the perfect date if you're constantly looking over their shoulder. Eventually, they'll be looking over their shoulder too, just to see what's behind them that's so interesting.

Even if the hottest person you've ever seen has entered the room and is giving you the eye, you have to ignore them and give your date the full attention they deserve.

Only in the following limited, and unlikely, circumstances are you permitted to look over your date's shoulder:

- ✔ A gunman has entered the room and is heading in your direction.

- ✔ A national lottery spokesperson is heading towards you with a cheque for £1 million with your name on it.

Chapter 18

(Almost) Ten Places where Unwanted Admirers may Strike

● ●

In This Chapter

▶ Putting space between yourself and colleagues

▶ Dealing with strangers

▶ Losing unwanted admirers

● ●

*O*ccasionally finding that your new best friend, colleague, or flirtation is actually very annoying can be disappointing. Worse still is when you find out they're actually pretty clingy and resistant to your polite efforts to let them down gently.

Most people have both the ability to tell when a relationship – romantic, work, as friends, or otherwise – isn't quite working and the sense to know when to walk away. Even if the object of your flirtation doesn't have this ability, then letting that person down gently is normally perfectly possible (see Chapter 11). Other people, though, can be clingier and more of a pest – whether they realise it or not – and just don't seem to get the message. People like this interpret your politeness and lack of obvious rejection as a positive reinforcement that you're actually enjoying their company and are keen to spend more time with them.

When someone lacks the degree of social etiquette that most people have, it can create an uneasy and unpleasant atmosphere with that person, so you need to spell out clearly what your feelings are towards them. Setting clear boundaries and being direct with someone isn't always easy, but helps you to deal with the problem. This chapter gives you ways of doing this in various flirting situations.

At Work

Although lots of flirting goes on in the workplace, it's never a good place to have an unwanted, clingy admirer, because you could potentially be stuck with them until you change jobs.

Several effective strategies for dealing with such a person in your workplace are to:

- ✔ Introduce them to someone who shares their interests or has something in common with them.
- ✔ Arrive at meetings last and sit out of eye contact with them.
- ✔ Pretend to work on something urgent until their lunchtime is almost up so that you have your own space during your lunch hour. This also cuts down the amount of time you both spend in the same place.

If the person giving you unwanted attention really won't get the message, tell them that you're not keen on fraternising with other people from the office. Remember, though, that this strategy only works if they don't see you hanging out with any other co-workers.

In a Bar

Unwanted admirers have a way of creeping up on you but in a bar they're quite easy to deal with. Try these lines for getting out of sticky flirting situations when you're out on the tiles:

- ✔ 'Excuse me, I just need to pop to the loo.' Make sure you finish your drink first, as you won't be returning and it'll be a shame to waste it.
- ✔ 'I'm supposed to be meeting a friend here; I'd better just go and look for them, as they're on their own.' This strategy doesn't work well in small bars, so consider pre-programming in a text from your friend saying they'll be with you in five minutes and then send it to yourself. Make your excuses and leave.

If they're very persistent, have a word with the bouncer to let them know they're making a nuisance of themselves and they'll be asked to leave before you know it!

While Networking

Networking events are great for a bit of flirting. Beware, though – you can find yourself the centre of attention for people who are so pleased they've found someone to talk to they'll stay welded to your side. With a bit of strategy on your part, however, not only are you able to extract yourself from their company, you can also benefit from the situation.

Ask them who are the most interesting and influential people that they know here and if they can introduce you to them. When you've got your introduction to the big cheese, return the favour and introduce your admirer to someone you know, then excuse yourself and get back to the big cheese. That way, you can both potentially benefit from having made each other's acquaintance – they've introduced you to someone and you've returned the favour. You can then get on with the business of networking with people you do actually want to be around.

Alternatively, you could try taking them to get a coffee. Lots of jostling is usually going on and you'll either be parted or a natural interruption of other people talking to you over the coffee table will occur. This gives you the opportunity to engage your new target in animated conversation and hopefully encourage the person you want to get away from to do the same – with a different target.

In the Street

Unwanted attention in the street can come in all shapes and sizes – someone wolf-whistling at you, a pedestrian brushing up against you as they sit down beside you on a street bench, or someone out on the town and under the influence, attempting to flirt with you as they walk between bars. At best, the unwanted attention can be irritating; at worst, it can be worrying and sometimes dangerous, especially if you're on your own.

No matter in what form the unwanted attention arrives, good manners and civility cost nothing, so rather than end up in a slanging match with them while they try to block your path or jog along the pavement with you, look them confidently in the eye and say very firmly 'I'm spoken for'. If they try and engage you in conversation, keep repeating the same phrase. Put some distance between you and them, preferably moving to the other side of the street rather than have them follow behind you, and make your way purposefully to somewhere you feel less intimidated by their behaviour, such as a crowded bar or street. Looking confident is king because the person is less likely to continue to bother you, seeking a weaker target instead.

In Your Circle of Friends

As much as you love your friends, unfortunately there often seems to be one who outstays their welcome, who wants to be more than just friends, or who doesn't get the message that you have a social life with other friends and don't wish to spend every waking moment with them.

If a certain friend is constantly texting, phoning, or emailing you wanting to know what you're doing, make a point of not responding to them immediately. Don't respond at all sometimes and always avoid responding to their questioning. Just because someone contacts you, doesn't mean you have to respond to them.

Try repeating the same line when declining their invitation to meet up, for example 'I'm sorry, I've got plans then'. Don't be drawn on what these plans are and just keep saying the same thing. Even the most persistent person will give up interrogating you when they realise they're going to get the same answer.

You may find treating your friend in this way difficult at first, but the sense of satisfaction from not having to explain your every move or include them in all your social activities far outweighs your initial discomfort.

On the Internet

You've met someone online and added them as a friend on Facebook. Then you become aware that they're following your every move and also, through you, those of your friends. You can rid yourself of a cyber stalker by removing them as a friend and adding them to your spam or black list so they can't email you either.

Don't forget to tell your friends who've added this person to their list of contacts about them, so they can't use your friends to continue spying on you.

If your cyber stalker remains persistent, contact Facebook or whichever social networking or dating site they're on and report them for inappropriate/antisocial behaviour. The site manager can then disable their account.

I can see you

Pat had a friend who wanted to be more than just friends with him, and who was constantly texting him and wanting to know what he was doing and who he was doing it with. The friend's behaviour was innocent enough to start with, but she began getting agitated if she didn't hear straight away what Pat was up to, or if he didn't report his precise movements. If she noticed Pat's car wasn't outside his house, she'd text him to say she'd noticed and what was he doing. She tried to cosy up to Pat's new friends, getting their numbers and texting them too. Pat started to feel as though he was being constantly watched. Filled with resentment, Pat started taking longer to respond to her texts and, when he did, refusing to give his where-abouts. His clingy friend started to get the message and Pat didn't feel so powerless in dealing with her.

Sidelining a clingy friend can be very distressing but having to put up with them is even more so. Spot the signs early and don't become their obsession.

At the Office Party

The office party provides the perfect venue for the person you've never even noticed before to make their move. You may find them following you around the room until they've had enough booze to give just the confidence booster they need to cling to you closer than a nylon nightie. Try the following:

- ✔ Make sure you have a friend on each arm as a human barrier, so they can't get physically close.

- ✔ Introduce them to someone you think fancies them and leave them to it.

- ✔ Tell them you're seeing someone else or that you fancy some-one else and don't want to jeopardise your chances by being seen flirting with them.

At the Gym

Being on the receiving end of unwanted, unshakable attention from someone at the gym can be most off-putting. Not only does this person ruin your workout, they add stress to a supposedly de-stressing situation.

Pick the strategy that suits you best to deal with the situation:

✔ Have a word at the reception desk and ask if this person comes to the gym at regular times – then avoid them.

✔ Do your workout back to front – if they're doing cardio, you do weights, and so on.

✔ Ask to have louder music in the gym or wear headphones.

✔ Offer one-word answers and tell them you're in a rush to get round as you're focusing on your workout or you're meeting someone afterwards.

On the Phone

Persistent telephone calls can be a real invasion of privacy. If an unwanted admirer obtains your telephone number – by fair means or foul – and begins to make a nuisance of themselves by repeatedly calling you, you need to nip the problem in the bud before it gets out of hand.

Being unpleasant isn't necessary; just ask the caller in a calm but decisive manner to stop calling you. If necessary, keep saying it over and over again. If the problem persists, tell the caller that you're going to report them to your telephone service provider, who can then help you to deal with the nuisance caller. You can also make use of services that display caller numbers on your phone and block certain callers and anonymous numbers from calling you.

Chapter 19

Ten Tips for Safe Flirting

....

In This Chapter

▶ Protecting your identity

▶ Meeting safely

▶ Having a plan B

▶ Protecting yourself

....

*Y*our mother told you never to speak to strangers, but now you're an adult you can just adopt safe strategies when flirting and dating. Always keep safety in the back of your mind whilst flirting, but don't worry about it so much that it prevents you from enjoying it. Be aware of these ten top tips to ensure that you can flirt with gay abandon and remain safe in the process.

Withhold Personal Information

Giving any of your key personal details away on an Internet site, or when corresponding with people you haven't met, is always a bad idea, particularly if you end up deciding you aren't interested in meeting them in person or you don't want to see them again.

 In any scenario where you don't know the individual you're flirting with, keep your work and home email address, postal address, and telephone numbers to yourself.

 Set up a free email address to use until you know them well enough to trust them with your personal contact details. If you're dating several people at once, invest in a pay-as-you-go mobile phone sim card so you have a separate telephone number for dates.

 If you're having a chance encounter flirting with a stranger and you or they want to meet, ask for their number so that you can control the flow of information and contact.

Arrange to Meet in a Public Place

Before speaking to your date about arranging a venue to meet, consider the following tips to pick the perfect spot for your flirting encounter and to ensure you meet as safely as possible:

- Never let a new date pick you up from your home or work address.
- Always meet in a public place.
- Pick a venue where you know lots of people will be around.

Take Your Flirting Slowly

Pacing your flirtation is important, particularly if you're flirting with someone from the office or a client. If your date has had a drink it may have loosened their inhibitions and they may want to move things on a bit faster than you're ready for.

Don't be rushed into anything. Flirting is a game for two people: if you're not playing, then they're harassing.

If you feel that they're moving too fast and you want to slow down, lessen eye contact and use the barrier technique (see Chapter 11) to put some space between you. If these hints still don't slow them down, put your backup plan into action. See the later section 'Have an Emergency Plan B'.

Drink with Caution

You don't drink and drive and you should apply the same health warning to flirting. Accepting drinks from strangers can be dangerous because they're easy to spike.

If you must accept a drink:

- Watch the bar staff pour it and take it from them directly.
- Ask for drinks in bottles and keep your thumb over the top.
- Never leave your drink unattended.
- Don't ask for a type of drink that you're unused to, because you won't be able to tell whether you feel peculiar simply because it's more potent than you're used to or because it's been spiked.
- Don't accept a drink that differs from the one you ordered.

If you think your drink has been spiked, inform one of the bar staff immediately and ask them to call a friend to arrange your safe passage home.

Watch What You Say

Discretion is the better part of valour. You have no way of guaranteeing what you say isn't going to go any further. So don't say anything about anyone that you wouldn't say to their face or that you wouldn't like said about you. This advice is particularly important if you're dating someone from work or who belongs to your circle of friends.

 If somebody's using excessive sexy talk or innuendo, don't laugh or smile politely if their words are making you uncomfortable. They may mistakenly think you're enjoying their banter and are ready to take things further.

Listen with Your Gut

Your gut has more nerve endings than your brain, so if you're clenched up, it's probably trying to tell you something. Victims of attack have often reported that they were aware of their gut instinct cutting in – but ignored it.

 If you have a gut feeling something's wrong, don't take any chances. Make your excuses and leave.

Keep Friends on Standby

Your friends care about you so they'll be more than happy to be on hand to check on you or bail you out. Ask a friend to call you at the beginning of the evening to check you've arrived safely and met your date and again at the end to check you're home safely.

 Have pre-prepared text messages ready on your mobile phone to send to your friends if things don't go to plan and you need to be bailed out. Pre-arrange that they'll come and pick you up and get you home safely.

Find Your Own Way Home

Even if you've had a great time together, don't be tempted to share a cab or a lift home. Save an invitation back for coffee for when you know the other person better and both parties' intentions and agendas are clear.

Pre-book a cab or arrange to travel home with friends after a date.

Have an Emergency Plan B

Follow the boy scouts and always be prepared. If you feel cornered in a situation you may feel anxious, vulnerable, and out of control. Having an emergency 'Plan B' is really only necessary in extreme circumstances, but having it up your sleeve keeps you flirting confidently and safely.

In preparation for any time that you don't feel comfortable, have an emergency text ready on your mobile phone to send to a friend for them to ring you in five minutes, and the number for a local cab firm so you can make a quick getaway. You can send a draft text easily from inside your handbag or pocket, or if you have to get away, quickly and discreetly call a cab from the toilet.

Learn Self-defence

Knowing how to defend yourself makes you feel more self-assured; it also boosts your confidence. Get yourself along to your local martial arts or self-defence class – you may even meet someone you fancy there!

In the unlikely and unfortunate event that you're attacked, scream 'Fire' as loudly as possible. Apparently, people are more likely to respond to this cry than anything else. A personal alarm may be useful to momentarily alarm your attacker and give you the chance to escape.

Index

interpreting signals. *See also* body language
  of availability, 82–86, 93, 211
  checking your skills, 133
  clues when someone likes you, 159
  clusters of clues for, 52, 158, 159
  confidence gained by, 13
  on dates, 51–52
  detective work for, 160
  eye versus body signals, 139
  factors masking mutual attraction, 207
  female flirting signals, 177–182
  of flirting with intent, 46–47
  importance for men, 11
  of interest, 86, 212
  linguistic clues, 108–109
  male flirting signals, 182–184
  mirroring, 152–158
  misinterpreting friendliness as sexual
    availability, 47
  misreading as pitfall of flirting, 12
  for office romance, 200
  order important in, 14
  people watching to learn, 13
  readiness to kiss, 193
  responses to conversation, 107–112
  Rule of four for, 158, 159
  smile types, 142–143
  smiles, fake versus real, 141
  uses for, 13
interrupting, avoiding, 115
intimate proximity zone, 134, 135, 136–137
intimidation
  from full-on stance, 189
  in office romance, 189, 190
  spatial dominance versus, 150
  from unwanted attention, 239–240
introduction icebreakers, 100
irritations, managing, 208

• *J* •

jaw drop when smiling, 142
joke telling, 38, 39, 103–104

• *K* •

kissing
  chemical connection during, 195
  cues for, 178, 193
  initiating, 193
  keeping bonds strong, 208

lip care for, 64
  sexual harassment issues, 53
Kuhnke, Elizabeth (*Body Language
    For Dummies*), 5

• *L* •

language. *See also* conversation
  mirroring, 119–120
  positive, 117–119
leaning away, 163
leaning in, 74, 110–111, 163
leaving them wanting more, 191–192
legs
  getting a limb in, 154
  twining by woman, 180
Lehu, Pierre (*Sex For Dummies*), 194
letting a person down. *See* rejecting
    advances
letting it all hang out, 163–164
life and soul of the party, 22
lighting, power spots affected by, 97
linguistic signals of interest, 108–109
lip salve, 64
lips
  brushing with fingers, 180
  female flirting signals, 178
  licking yours before kissing, 195
  tight-lipped smiles, 142
lipstick, red, 181
list agencies, 90
listening
  leaning in during, 74, 110–111
  letting others talk, 120, 121
  for showing interest, 116
  with your gut, 245
long-term relationships
  basis for, 207–208
  factors masking mutual attraction, 207
  minor irritations in, 208
  showing love in, 208
look. *See* appearance
looking over their shoulder, avoiding, 235
love, 207, 208. *See also* office romance
lying
  body language indicating, 169–172
  compulsive, 170
  conversation clues indicating, 172–173
  disentangling from liars, 173–174
  flattery, 170
  white lies, 170

• *V* •

Notes

FOR DUMMIES®

Making Everything Easier!™

UK editions

BUSINESS

978-0-470-51806-9 Starting a Business

978-0-470-77930-9 Competitive Strategy

978-0-470-71382-2 Consulting

FINANCE

978-0-470-99280-7 Investing

978-0-470-99811-3 Tax

978-0-470-69515-9 Sorting Out Your Finances

HOBBIES

978-0-470-69960-7 Growing Your Own Fruit & Veg

978-0-470-77085-6 Backgammon

978-0-470-75857-1 Origami Kit

Body Language For Dummies
978-0-470-51291-3

British Sign Language
For Dummies
978-0-470-69477-0

Business NLP For Dummies
978-0-470-69757-3

Cricket For Dummies
978-0-470-03454-5

Digital Marketing For Dummies
978-0-470-05793-3

Divorce For Dummies, 2nd Edition
978-0-470-74128-3

eBay.co.uk For Dummies,
2nd Edition
978-0-470-51807-6

English Grammar For Dummies
978-0-470-05752-0

Fertility & Infertility For Dummies
978-0-470-05750-6

Genealogy Online For Dummies
978-0-7645-7061-2

Golf For Dummies
978-0-470-01811-8

Green Living For Dummies
978-0-470-06038-4

Hypnotherapy For Dummies
978-0-470-01930-6

Inventing For Dummies
978-0-470-51996-7

Lean Six Sigma For Dummies
978-0-470-75626-3

FOR DUMMIES®

A world of resources to help you grow

UK editions

SELF-HELP

Cognitive Behavioural Therapy For Dummies
978-0-470-01838-5

Neuro-linguistic Programming For Dummies
978-0-7645-7028-5

Emotional Freedom Technique For Dummies
978-0-470-75876-2

HEALTH

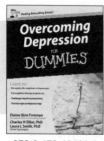
Overcoming Depression For Dummies
978-0-470-69430-5

IBS For Dummies
978-0-470-51737-6

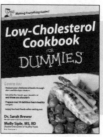
Low-Cholesterol Cookbook For Dummies
978-0-470-71401-0

HISTORY

British History For Dummies
978-0-470-99468-9

Twentieth Century History For Dummies
978-0-470-51015-5

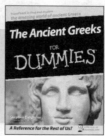
The Ancient Greeks For Dummies
978-0-470-98787-2

Motivation For Dummies
978-0-470-76035-2

Personal Development All-In-One For Dummies
978-0-470-51501-3

PRINCE2 For Dummies
978-0-470-51919-6

Psychometric Tests For Dummies
978-0-470-75366-8

Raising Happy Children For Dummies
978-0-470-05978-4

Reading the Financial Pages For Dummies
978-0-470-71432-4

Starting and Running a Business All-in-One For Dummies
978-0-470-51648-5

Succeeding at Assessment Centres For Dummies
978-0-470-72101-8

Sudoku For Dummies
978-0-470-01892-7

Teaching Skills For Dummies
978-0-470-74084-2

Time Management For Dummies
978-0-470-77765-7

Understanding and Paying Less Property Tax For Dummies
978-0-470-75872-4

Wills, Probate, & Inheritance Tax For Dummies, 2nd Edition
978-0-470-75629-4

Work-Life Balance For Dummies
978-0-470-71380-8

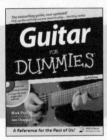

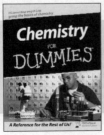

FOR DUMMIES®

Helping you expand your horizons and achieve your potential

COMPUTER BASICS

978-0-470-27759-1

978-0-470-13728-4

978-0-471-75421-3

DIGITAL LIFESTYLE

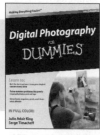

978-0-470-25074-7

978-0-470-39062-7

978-0-470-42342-4

WEB & DESIGN

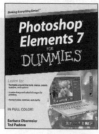

978-0-470-39700-8

978-0-470-32725-8

978-0-470-34502-3
